HAMLET

NOTES

including
- Date of Composition
- The Texts
- The Source
- An Introduction to Interpretations
- Summaries and Commentaries
- Review Questions
- Selected Bibliography

by
James K. Lowers, Ph.D.
Department of English
University of Hawaii

INCORPORATED
LINCOLN, NEBRASKA   68501

Editor

Gary Carey, M.A.
University of Colorado

Consulting Editor

James L. Roberts, Ph.D.
Department of English
University of Nebraska

ISBN 0-8220-0018-0
© Copyright 1971
by
C. K. Hillegass
All Rights Reserved
Printed in U.S.A.

1993 Printing

Cliffs Notes, Inc.   Lincoln, Nebraska

CONTENTS

Hamlet Notes

DATE OF COMPOSITION

An entry in the Stationers' Register (in which were recorded works authorized for publication in accordance with the royal charter granted to printers) under the date July 26, 1602, reads: "A booke called the Revenge of Hamlett Prince Denmarke as yt was latelie Acted by the Lord Chamberleyne his servantes." Although some scholars are content to accept the year 1602 as the date of composition, the consensus is that it had been composed earlier. A few would push the date back to 1598, since Gabriel Harvey, one of Shakespeare's contemporaries, made reference to *Hamlet* in a note which he wrote in his copy of Speght's *Chaucer* (1598). Certainly Shakespeare's play could not have been known before that year because it is not included among the plays listed by Francis Meres in *Palladis Tamia,* which also was published in 1598. But it does not necessarily follow that Harvey wrote his interesting note in the year in which Speght's *Chaucer* was published. Most students of Shakespeare accept late 1600 or early 1601 as the date of publication.

By the year 1601, Shakespeare had written no less than ten comedies, nine chronicle histories, and three tragedies other than *Hamlet*. But it is *The Tragedy of Hamlet* which marks the beginning of the playwright's great period of composition. *Hamlet* itself belongs with *Othello* (1604), *King Lear* (1605/6), and *Macbeth* (1606) as one of the greatest tragedies in world literature. Many informed students of Shakespeare insist that it is his greatest play.

THE TEXTS

Sound commentary on *Hamlet,* scene by scene, calls for some knowledge of the first three published versions of the play; two of these appeared during his lifetime and the third appeared seven years after his death. In 1603 the First Quarto, unauthorized by the author or his company, was published. The title read: "The Tragicall Historie of Hamlet Prince of Denmark by William Shakespeare. As it hath been diverse times acted by his Highnesse servants in the Cittie of London: as also in the two Vniuersities of Cambridge and Oxford." There are two points of immediate interest here: (1) the Lord Chamberlain's

Company, of which Shakespeare was a member, had become the King's Servants upon the ascension of James I; (2) *The Tragedy of Hamlet* apparently had an intellectual appeal from the start, as the performances at the universities indicate.

The First Quarto is a quite garbled version of Shakespeare's tragedy, although it contains some 240 lines not found in the next version of the play. This earlier printed version just possibly represents *Hamlet* in a transitional stage of composition, but it is practically worthless as a text.

In 1604 the Second Quarto edition of *Hamlet* was published. It is this text, with certain minor additions and corrections, which is generally acknowledged to be Shakespeare's definitive version. Further, it is the Second Quarto which, according to eminent scholars, served as the source for the version included in the First Folio (1623), the latter being essentially an acting version necessarily cut by more than 200 lines, although some new passages were added. Good modern texts of *The Tragedy of Hamlet,* therefore, depend overwhelmingly on the Second Quarto.

THE SOURCE

Sound commentary on this tragedy also calls for a knowledge of the sources available to Shakespeare when he decided to dramatize the story of Hamlet, Prince of Denmark. Time and again, critics have turned to an earlier version or versions in their efforts to find answers to questions which inevitably arise. Moreover, knowledge of earlier versions makes possible a surer appreciation of Shakespeare's accomplishment.

The story of Hamlet goes far back in Scandinavian legend, in this respect bearing comparison with the Anglo-Saxon account of Beowulf. The earliest surviving literary tale of Hamlet is found in Saxo Grammaticus' *Historia Danica* (c. 1200). For his *Histoires Tragiques* (1576), a widely popular collection of tales in French, Francois de Belleforest adopted it, with basic themes, prototypes of characters, and story elements later to be found in Shakespeare's play. These include adultery, fratricide, revenge, assumed madness, and the villain's use of spies and especially of the girl loved by the hero. Nevertheless, the differences between Belleforest's version and Shakespeare's are great and significant. The chief ones in the former are as follows:

1. The action takes place in pre-Christian times, and the standards of morality and conduct differ accordingly.

2. The slaying of King Hamlet is public knowledge, although the usurping murderer succeeds in convincing the public that he acted only in defense of the Queen.

3. Hamlet is depicted as a defenseless youth who pretends to be mad in order to protect himself.

4. Although Hamlet is dedicated to truth, he emerges as being vindictively cruel.

5. As in Saxo Grammaticus, Hamlet's manifestations of madness take rather absurd forms, a notable example being his crowing like a cock and flailing his arms.

6. The Queen sincerely repents, and Hamlet tells her that he plans to kill her villainous husband.

7. Hamlet marries the daughter of the King of Britain and remains in England for a full year.

8. Hamlet returns to Denmark just as his uncle is celebrating the young Prince's own death.

9. Hamlet succeeds in getting all the courtiers drunk and then sets fire to the palace and kills the King.

If this were the only version of the Hamlet story available to Shakespeare, critics would have no more difficulty as regards source than they have in dealing with *Othello,* the source for which is just one story. But there was written and performed in England an earlier Hamlet play, usually referred to as the *Ur-Hamlet,* which unfortunately has not survived in manuscript or print.

The *Ur-Hamlet* dates before 1589, for in that year Thomas Nashe made a reference to it. The general opinion is that the *Ur-Hamlet* was the work of Thomas Kyd, best known for the widely popular *The Spanish Tragedy* (printed in 1594), a tragedy replete with a ghost and sensational incidents, in which a father takes vengeance on his son's murderer. A diary entry made by Philip Henslowe, an Elizabethan theatrical manager, tells us that this *Hamlet* was acted on June 11, 1594, by members of the Lord Admiral's Men and the Lord Chamberlain's Men, the latter being the group of which Shakespeare was a member. A third reference is found in Thomas Lodge's *Wit's Misery* (1596).

What conclusions are to be made from all this? First, when Shakespeare's *Hamlet* was first presented, the audience was already familiar with a Hamlet story, one in which revenge is the dominant theme. Second, since the *Ur-Hamlet* apparently belonged to the popular Senecan tradition of the Elizabethan stage and has been generally attributed to Thomas Kyd, *The Spanish Tragedy,* which survives, must be a prototype. In that play are found the pagan revengeful ghost, the protagonist's unceasing efforts to attain vengeance, his intermittent madness, and extreme sensationalism. Kyd properly is credited with dramatic skill in plot construction, for he carefully provides motivation and suspense before moving to the catastrophe, or resolution. What especially is missing is the intellectual probing, the apparently studied ambiguity, the complexity of character portrayal, the superior poetry—all of which are to be found in Shakespeare's play. One may assume that the popular *Ur-Hamlet* sufficed insofar as melodrama is concerned; Shakespeare had to transcend the melodramatic, imbuing the material with new significance and interest without sacrificing the sheer excitement of the action.

THE PLAY: AN INTRODUCTION TO INTERPRETATIONS

Although many students of Shakespeare believe that *Hamlet*, among all the plays in the Shakespearean canon, best reflects the universality of the poet-dramatist's genius, it remains an enigmatical work, what has been called a "grand poetical puzzle." No artist can control the use to which his insights are put by posterity, and this dictum is especially true of Shakespeare, whose Hamlet has caused more discussion than any other character in fiction, dramatic or non-dramatic.

Many readers have been disturbed by what has been called the "two Hamlets in the play": one, the sensitive young intellectual and idealist, the "sweet prince" who expresses himself in unforgettable poetry and who is dedicated to truth; the other, a barbaric Hamlet who treats Ophelia so cruelly, who slays Polonius and then speaks of lugging the guts into another room, and who callously reports sending Rosencrantz and Guildenstern to their deaths. It has been argued that Shakespeare transmuted an old play without reconstructing it in response to audiences who would not have tolerated excisions (J. M. Robertson, *"Hamlet" Once More*, London, 1923).

Most commentators cannot accept this argument. For one thing, audiences and readers find themselves very sympathetic to Hamlet—some even to the extent of identifying with him. But if there are those who create Hamlet in their own images, fortunately others have sought to find the key to his character through intensive study of Renaissance thought. Yet no answer that satisfies all, or even most, has been found. In the words of a competent Shakespearean critic of the last century, H. N. Hudson, "It is easy to invent with plausibility almost any theory respecting [Hamlet], but very hard to make any theory comprehend the whole subject" (Introduction to *Hamlet*, 1870). Some familiarity with leading theories regarding the tragic hero is necessary if the commentaries provided scene by scene in these Notes are to prove most useful.

Most interpreters of *Hamlet* start with the assumption that the tragic hero has a clear and sacred obligation to kill Claudius and to do so without delay. The basic question, then, is why does so much time elapse before the young Prince sweeps to his revenge? It is argued that, if Hamlet had substituted prompt action for the considerable verbalism in which he repeatedly berates himself for procrastination, Gertrude, Polonius, Ophelia, Rosencrantz, Guildenstern, Laertes, and—most important—Hamlet himself would have survived. But then Shakespeare would not have achieved tragedy and the resulting work would have been no more than a potboiler. There must be found some effective explanation for Hamlet's long delay.

HAMLET, THE VICTIM OF EXTERNAL DIFFICULTIES

Before one turns to the more elaborate and better-known theories, it is desirable to notice one that provides a simple answer: as is true in Belleforest's prose version of the story, the Hamlet of Shakespeare's play faces external difficulties which make immediate, positive action impossible. Claudius was too powerful and only once before the final scene placed himself in a defenseless position. Moreover, had the Prince been able to carry out the Ghost's injunction of immediate revenge, he would have placed himself in an especially difficult position. How could he have convinced the people that he justifiably had executed revenge? To be sure, this theory leaves many questions unanswered. But, as will be true with reference to other theories, no rebuttal is required here and now.

HAMLET, THE SENTIMENTAL DREAMER

Leading Romantic critics of the late eighteenth and early nineteenth centuries saw Hamlet as a young man, attractive and gifted in many ways, but incapable of positive action. For them, "the native hue of resolution/Is sicklied o'er with the pale cast of thought," to use Hamlet's own words (III.i.84-85). One would have little difficulty in finding several passages in the play which seem to support such an interpretation. These will be noted in the commentaries.

Goethe is to be credited with first providing in detail this basically sentimental interpretation. His Hamlet is a young man of "lovely, pure, and moral nature, without the strength of nerve which forms a hero." In brief, Goethe's Prince of Denmark is an impractical dreamer. Some thirty years later, A. W. Schleger, Goethe's compatriot, arrived at the same conclusion. His Hamlet has "no firm belief either in himself or in anything else. . . . in the resolutions which he so often embraces and always leaves unexecuted, his weakness is too apparent. . . . his far-fetched scruples are often mere pretexts to cover his want of determination. . . ." *(Dramatic Art and Literature,* 1810).

Leading English Romantics arrived at the same conclusion. Coleridge's well-known remarks on the character of Hamlet have been most influential. For him, the Prince of Denmark suffers from an "over-balance of the contemplative faculty" and, like any man, "thereby becomes the creature of mere meditation and loses his power to action" *(Notes and Lectures on Shakespeare,* 1808). And William Hazlitt continues: "At other times, when he is most bound to act, he remains puzzled, undecided, and sceptical, dallies with his purposes, till the occasion is lost, and finds out some pretense to relapse into indolence and thoughtfulness again" *(Characters in Shakespeare's Plays,* 1818).

That this Romantic view of Hamlet has survived into the twentieth century is only too evident. The late Arthur Quiller-Couch stated: "Hamlet's character is the prevalence of the abstracting and generalizing habit over the practical. . . . He is full of purpose, but void of that quality of mind which accomplishes purpose" *(Shakespeare's Workmanship,* 1931).

HAMLET, THE VICTIM OF EXCESSIVE MELANCHOLY

Traditionally, Hamlet has been called the Melancholy Dane, and quite appropriately. His first lines in Act I, Scene ii, wherein he first appears, and certainly his first long soliloquy establish him as grief-stricken. Moreover, Hamlet himself refers to melancholy in a way which suggests that it is a debilitating factor. Ordinary grief, of course, is one thing; everyone experiences it. But Hamlet's grief, it is argued, is pathological; it is a destructive thing which causes him to procrastinate and leads to his death. Actually, this theory dates from the eighteenth century. Among later critics who have accepted it is A. C. Bradley, whose still widely influential Oxford lectures on Shakespeare's tragedies were first published in 1904. In a definite way his work represents the keystone in the arch of Romantic criticism because he treats Hamlet not as *dramatis persona,* not as an artistic representation which stops just where the author chooses, but as a living human being. Again like the early nineteenth-century Romantics, Bradley found Hamlet to be irresolute. He makes reference to what he calls Hamlet's "otiose think-ing which hardly deserves the name of thought, an unconscious weaving of pretexts for inaction." At the root of this, Bradley finds melancholy which was "increased by deepening self-contempt."

Melancholy has been called the "Elizabethan malady." It was recognized as a disease and was the subject of treatises published in England and on the Continent. At the time Shakespeare wrote *Hamlet,* Timothy Bright's *A Treatise of Melancholie,* first published in 1586, was well known. In an age when the proper study of mankind was man, it seems improbable that a writer like Shakespeare, with his manifest intellectual curiosity and acquisitive mind, was unfamiliar with con-temporary ideas regarding the causes, symptoms, and results of mel-ancholy. Indeed, melancholy characters of one kind or another appeared rather often in Elizabethan and Jacobean plays. Hamlet, inevitably, has been classified as the intellectual melancholy type. The disease which afflicts him is the most destructive kind, namely, melancholy adust. When Hamlet speaks of "my weakness and my melancholy" (II.ii.630), for example; when he speaks "wild and whirling words" (I.v.133); when his mood shifts from deep depression to elation, he is following the pattern of behavior peculiar to the melancholic as described by Bright and other writers on the subject. So goes the argument.

HAMLET, THE VICTIM OF THE OEDIPUS COMPLEX

The Freudian, or neo-Freudian, interpretation of *Hamlet* appeals to many people today. The first and most elaborate presentation of this theory was made by Dr. Ernest Jones, disciple and biographer of Sig-mund Freud, as early as 1910 and received full expression in *Hamlet and Oedipus* (New York, 1949). Concisely stated, the Freudian inter-preters fervently believe that the Prince of Denmark suffered from the Oedipus complex — an undue and unhealthy attachment of a son for his mother which is apt to be morbidly suppressed and cause great mental distress. To quote Mr. Harry Levin, this ingenious theory "motivates Hamlet's delay by identifying him with Claudius, through whom he has vicariously accomplished the Oedipal feat of murdering his father and marrying his mother" *(The Question of Hamlet,* New York, p. 56). Mr. Levin rejects this theory.

HAMLET, MOTIVATED BY AMBITION

A few commentators see *The Tragedy of Hamlet* as one of the Elizabethan ambition plays. For them, the primary reason for Hamlet's desire to kill his uncle is not to avenge his father's "foul and most un-natural murder," but rather to make possible his own advancement to the throne. The delays and inner conflicts are the result of his aware-ness that personal ambition and pride, not sacred duty, motivate him. Once more it is possible to cite lines from the text which, if taken out of context, lend support to this theory.

HAMLET, MISLED BY THE GHOST

Not all critics agree that the Ghost of Hamlet's father is an "honest ghost" or that Hamlet himself has a solemn duty to slay Claudius. This, of course, is to deny the widely held assumption that the Prince was called upon to execute public justice — that he functions as God's min-ister, not as scourge who, though he may be the instrument of divine vengeance, is himself a grievous sinner and must suffer for his sins. For these critics, Shakespeare depicts a tragic hero who should not take vengeance into his own hands: not only Gertrude — but also Claudius — should be left to heaven.

To do full justice to the immediate subject, one should investigate in depth Renaissance theories of revenge. For the immediate purpose, let it be noted that Hamlet has been said to have been misled by the Ghost, the test of whose honesty is not the establishment of Claudius' guilt but rather the nature of its injunction. It is argued that the Prince is called upon to execute *private* vengeance, an eye for an eye, a tooth for a tooth, contrary to all Christian teaching. His problem, then, is that of a man who believes in heaven and hell and whose reason tells him that the man who defies divine ordinance ultimately must face judg-ment. It follows that Shakespeare portrays a tragic hero who should *not* take vengeance into his own hands and a Ghost that is "a spirit damn'd." This theory has been developed brilliantly by Miss Eleanor Prosser in her well-documented study, *Hamlet and Revenge* (Stanford Univer-sity Press, 1967). Certainly there are passages in the text of the play which may be used to establish vindictiveness in Hamlet's character. Instead of seeing Hamlet as one whose propensity for thought prevents him from performing the necessary action, Miss Prosser finds him to be one whose conscience, which operates with reason, restrains him for some time from acting impulsively in response to instinct.

From this survey of better-known interpretations of *Hamlet*, two major conclusions can be made. First, Shakespeare's tragedy is a work of surpassing interest and genius, and the tragic hero is universally attractive and fascinating. Second, only the naive will start with the assumption that there is one obvious interpretation of the play and that critics, not Shakespeare, have introduced complexities into it. It would be gratifying to be able to offer these Notes with the subtitle "The Meaning of *Hamlet*" and to present a simple, direct interpretation based upon a major generalization and to ignore passages in the play which do not fit into the argument. But such a presentation would not do justice to a great play or help the student. Therefore, when appropriate, passages which seem to lend support to a given theory will be called to the student's attention. But always one must ask himself whether or not the entire play urges the acceptance of such a theory; ultimately, major themes emerge from the entire plot, not from isolated episodes or passages.

All textual references are made to W. A. Neilson and C. J. Hill, *The Complete Plays and Poems of William Shakespeare*, The Riverside Press, Cambridge, Mass., 1942.

LIST OF CHARACTERS

Hamlet, Prince of Denmark

Son of the dead King Hamlet and nephew to the present ruler of Denmark; he has returned to Elsinore because of his father's death.

Claudius, King of Denmark

Hamlet's uncle who succeeded his brother to the throne and married his brother's wife.

Gertrude

Queen of Denmark and mother of Hamlet.

Polonius

Elderly Lord Chamberlain and thus chief counselor to Claudius.

Horatio

Commoner who is a fellow student and loyal friend of Hamlet.

Laertes

Polonius' son, a student at the University of Paris who, like Hamlet, has returned to Elsinore because of King Hamlet's death.

Ophelia

Obedient daughter of Polonius and sister of Laertes; the young court lady who Gertrude hoped would be Hamlet's bride.

Rosencrantz
Guildenstern
} One-time schoolfellows and friends of Hamlet.

Fortinbras

Prince of Norway, a valiant young man who, like Hamlet, has lost a father.

Osric

Affected courtier who plays a minor role as the King's messenger and as umpire of the fencing match between Hamlet and Laertes.

Voltimand
Cornelius
} Danish courtiers who are sent as ambassadors to the Court of Norway.

Marcellus
Bernardo
} Danish officers on guard at the castle of Elsinore.

Francisco

Danish soldier on guard duty at the castle of Elsinore.

Reynaldo

Young man whom Polonius instructs and sends to Paris to observe and report on Laertes' conduct.

The Gravediggers

Two clowns who dig Ophelia's grave, the first of whom is engaged by Hamlet in a grimly humorous conversation.

SUMMARIES AND COMMENTARIES

ACT I – SCENE 1

Summary

The setting is the royal castle at Elsinore. On a platform before the castle, Francisco, a soldier on guard duty, challenges Bernardo, an officer, who appears to relieve Francisco at midnight. Francisco expresses his thanks, for it is "bitter cold" and he is "sick at heart." Horatio and Marcellus, who are to join Bernardo in the watch, arrive and identify themselves as loyal Danes. "What, has this thing appear'd tonight?" asks Marcellus, and it is revealed that a strange, frightening apparition was seen during the watch on a previous occasion. Horatio, who has not seen it, has assured Marcellus that it is a hallucination but, at the officer's entreaty, has agreed to join in the watch.

As Bernardo is telling Horatio how the specter had appeared one hour after midnight, the Ghost itself enters. It is "like the King that's dead" – that is, it appears in the "fair and warlike form" of the late King Hamlet of Denmark. Marcellus urges Horatio to question it, but when Horatio charges the Ghost in heaven's name to speak, the apparition stalks away. The pale and trembling Horatio admits that it is "something more than fantasy."

In the ensuing discussion, one learns that the Ghost has appeared twice before in the same armor King Hamlet wore when he fought the ambitious old Fortinbras, King of Norway, and when he defeated the Poles. Further, in accordance with the solemn agreement made by the two contestants, King Hamlet won Norwegian territory when he defeated and slew his adversary. Now the dead king's son and namesake, young Fortinbras, has raised a force of men willing to fight only for subsistence and is determined to take back the lands his father lost. Thus the military preparations and the nightly watch at Elsinore are explained. Bernardo suggests that the Ghost's appearance may be a portent relating to the martial threat, and Horatio recalls the terrifying omens which preceded the assassination of Julius Caesar.

Again the Ghost appears, and again Horatio courageously challenges it to speak. But at the crow of a cock, it moves from one place to another and then departs. All agree that Hamlet, son of the King whose spirit they may have seen, must be told.

Commentary

First to be noted is the skill with which Shakespeare evokes a mood appropriate to this tragedy. The members of the guard appear in the bitter cold of a northern winter night. Francisco welcomes relief, although his has been a "quiet guard." His feeling of sickness at heart suggests that neither the hour nor the weather explains his uneasiness.

"Long live the king!" exclaims Bernardo, voicing the password when he is challenged by Francisco. "What king?" one asks; and as details relating to Denmark are provided, it seems to be evident that the changing of the guard is symbolic, "a re-enactment of those dynastic changes which frame the play" (H. Levin, p. 20). Support for such a conclusion is found in Horatio's words when he first addresses the Ghost as one "that usurp'st this time of night" (46).

What of the Ghost, "this thing . . . this dreaded sight," as Marcellus calls it, which fills Horatio with "fear and wonder"? Some knowledge of Elizabethan and Jacobean ghost-lore is needed. Shakespeare may or may not have believed in ghosts; the characters in this play do, and so did most of his contemporaries, including James I. The prevailing theories were that a ghost may be (1) a hallucination, (2) a spirit returned to perform some deed left undone in life, (3) a specter seen as a portent, (4) a spirit returned from the grave or from purgatory by divine permission, or (5) a devil disguised as a dead person. In the course of the play each of these theories is put to test. Immediately the first is rejected, but much later in the play it will arise again. The educated, skeptical Horatio proves to his own satisfaction that this particular ghost is a real one, not an illusion. Appearing in "warlike form" and as the image of the late King Hamlet, the second may be applicable or, more probably, the third, since Denmark expects an attack led by the young Norwegian Prince, Fortinbras. Horatio dwells upon this latter possibility when he speaks of the portents seen just before Julius Caesar was slain in the Roman Forum.

But Horatio and members of the guard particularly fear that the Ghost is diabolical. Horatio properly is called upon to question it because he is a scholar (42), trained in Latin and knowledgeable in arcane things. Among the mortals in this scene, only he is qualified to exorcise an evil spirit. As dawn, heralded by the cock's crow, begins to break and light begins to replace darkness, the Ghost "started like a guilty thing" (148). Marcellus is reminded that, according to a tradition accepted by many, the "bird of dawning singeth all night long" during the Christmas season and then "no spirit can walk abroad" (158 ff.). Indeed this apparition may be a thing of evil.

Significantly, *The Tragedy of Hamlet* is given a Christian setting from the start. Not only is reference made to "our Saviour's birth" in Marcellus' speech, but also Horatio uses the proper Christian formula in challenging the Ghost: "By heaven I charge thee, speak!" (49) – and his words, according to Marcellus, offend the Ghost, which stalks away.

The possibility still remains, however, that it is a spirit divinely sanctioned to return in order to carry out some mission.

One does not yet meet young Fortinbras, but what is learned about him is sufficiently interesting. He is a young man "of unproved mettle," one who has recently lost a royal father and who is not content to brood over his loss. Swiftly he has raised a force of "landless resolutes" — a gang of adventurers — and is determined to regain the territory which his father lost in combat.

ACT I – SCENE 2

Summary

In a room of state at Elsinore, King Claudius and Queen Gertrude enter, accompanied by Lord Chamberlain Polonius, his son Laertes, and various members of the Court and attendants. The King addresses all present. First, he speaks of mourning the death of his "dear brother," King Hamlet, and explains that "discretion" prohibits excessive grief. He has married his brother's widow and has done so with the concurrence of the members of his council. Next, he speaks about young Fortinbras, who demands the surrender of those lands lost by his father to King Hamlet. Claudius informs the Court that he is sending Cornelius and Voltimand with a letter to the bedridden King of Norway, requesting him to restrain his nephew.

Having concluded official business, Claudius listens to the suit of Laertes, who requests "leave and favour" to return to France after having returned to Denmark to attend the coronation ceremonies. The King first determines that Laertes has his father's permission and then graciously gives his own.

Claudius now turns to young Hamlet and asks why he still grieves. Queen Gertrude joins the King in urging her son to accept his father's death philosophically and to recognize that his own bereavement is not unique. After Hamlet assures his mother that he has not assumed a pose for effect, Claudius develops Gertrude's argument: it is "sweet and commendable" for Hamlet to show love for a dead father through immediate grief, but sustained grief is unmanly and evidence of "impious stubbornness." The Queen urges her son to remain at Elsinore. When Hamlet replies that he will strive to obey her, the King commends him. As Claudius and the Queen prepare to leave, the King announces that a celebration, replete with drink and the thunder of cannon, will be held in honor of Hamlet's "gentle and unforc'd accord" (123). All but the Prince leave the room.

Alone, Hamlet expresses his innermost thoughts. Were it not against God's law, he would commit suicide, for his world has become "weary, stale, flat, and unprofitable." But it is not just the death of a beloved father and king which has reduced him to this state of despair; it is the fact that his mother has married a man much inferior to King Hamlet, a man who was her brother-in-law, and has done so less than two months after her husband's death.

Horatio, in the company of Marcellus and Bernardo, enters. When he greets Hamlet, the young Prince, lost in his thoughts, makes a perfunctory reply. But promptly he recognizes Horatio and warmly returns the greeting. Horatio explains that he has returned from Wittenberg to attend the funeral of Hamlet's father. The Prince then asks Horatio not to mock him, remarking that his friend must have returned to attend the Queen's marriage to Claudius. Horatio concedes that little time elapsed between the funeral and the marriage.

Fervently, Hamlet expresses his regret that the marriage has taken place. Then, when he tells Horatio that he thinks he sees his father, Horatio is startled. "Oh, where, my lord?" he asks. Hamlet explains that he evoked imaginatively the image of the dead king. This provides Horatio the opportunity to report what he and the guards saw the night before—"A figure like your father,/ Arm'd at all points exactly" (199-200). Hamlet questions his friend closely and concludes that, come what may, he will accost the apparition. Both Horatio and Marcellus swear to honor Hamlet's injunction of silence regarding whatever may happen. Alone once more, the Prince expresses his conviction that the Ghost, apparelled like his father, is an omen that "All is not well."

Commentary

Claudius, who emerges as the antagonist, is first heard and calls for first attention. It should be obvious that here is no weak individual, but one who is adroit and determined. He is fully aware that his marriage to Gertrude is incestuous according to canon law, which is based on the dictum that man and wife become one flesh. He knows further that the marriage, even were it lawful, took place with undue haste. Typically, royal periods of mourning last for a full year; this marriage took place less than two months after the death of Claudius' brother. But this new ruler has taken care to obtain the approval of his Court. How he was able to do so in the face of canon law is revealed by his carefully chosen words in the first twenty-five lines of his opening speech, concluding with "So much for him." Notice the skillfully balanced phrases, the careful parallelisms, the antitheses which he employs as he rationalizes his act. Discretion (reason) is set against grief and nature; Gertrude is referred to first as "sometime sister," then as Queen, and finally as "imperial jointress" of Denmark. The effect is to convince his audience that he has been motivated by a high sense of public duty.

When he turns to state affairs, Claudius is no less confident, and one must concede that he exhibits decisiveness and capability as a ruler. Although Denmark fears an invasion led by young Fortinbras, the Court and the people in general may rest assured that their King has taken proper action. Claudius appears to show tact for all concerned when he ascertains that Polonius will not oppose his son's departure. King Claudius' public image is a favorable one.

Nor does it appear to diminish when he turns to Hamlet. But again the careful reader will note that, in addressing the Prince as "my cousin [kinsman] Hamlet, and my son," Claudius adroitly makes clear the fact that he is in full command and that Hamlet is subject to his pleasure. Once more it is an appeal to reason that seems to color the King's words as he reproves his nephew for undue grief and urges him to embrace forgetfulness. On strict philosophical and religious grounds, his argument is impeccable. All mankind must bow to the inevitable and learn to accept it, for life in general must go on. From this point of view, continued and debilitating sorrow is indeed "a fault to heaven,/A fault against the dead, a fault to nature" (101-2).

When Claudius accuses Hamlet of "impious stubbornness" (94), of possessing "A heart unfortified" and "a mind impatient" and "An understanding simple and unschool'd" (96-97), he is saying, in so many words, that the Prince lacks the qualities required to rule a kingdom. Thus the King may well intend to strengthen the belief of the Danish counselors that it was best for Claudius to succeed his brother. Certainly the King's words have a declamatory quality which suggests that he knows that Gertrude and the members of the Court also hear his words.

Claudius' call for a celebration with festive drink is, in effect, an order that Hamlet especially, and all others, forget the past and accept the new order. Some commentators (Samuel Johnson, for example) have argued that the King's intemperance, suggested here, is strongly impressed in the play. If this be true, Claudius' appetite for strong drink, according to Renaissance moral philosophy, points to his rejection of reason, which is equated with virtue. But admittedly the evidence to support such a conclusion is rather slight at this stage of the action.

Nothing that Queen Gertrude says or does in this scene informs against her except the fact that she is obviously undisturbed by her new status as wife to Claudius. Her concern for her son seems to be that of a genuinely concerned mother. If Claudius' words tend to arouse suspicions as to his true motives, not so Gertrude's. Her plea, "Let not thy mother lose her prayers, Hamlet" (118), has the ring of sincerity. It is not until one hears the Prince speak in soliloquy that Gertrude takes her place, as it were, among the unsympathetic characters. Far more serious than the *haste* of the marriage to Claudius is the fact that it is incestuous:

her marriage to her brother-in-law was a gross violation of the law of the Church. Hamlet's indictment of his mother may provide the key to her character—weakness manifested by sensual passion:

> Must I remember? Why, she would hang on him
> As if increase of appetite had grown
> By what it fed on. . . .
>
> (143-45)

Present also in this scene is Laertes, who speaks just less than seven lines. He appears as the well-bred son of the Lord Chamberlain, observing the amenities appropriate to his station and the occasion. More significant is one's reaction to his father, Polonius, chief counselor to the King, although he speaks just four lines. Just as there is a contrived element apparent in Claudius' first speech, so there is an artificiality in that of Polonius. The adjective, it has been said, can be the enemy of the noun. Polonius loves adjectives. Note the pattern of his discourse: ". . . *slow* leave . . . *laboursome* petition . . . *hard* consent" (58-60). This hardly suggests naturalness or spontaneity.

But the play belongs to Hamlet. Almost everything other characters do or say is relevant primarily to him. His tragedy is already in progress when he first appears. In this way he provides a contrast to the usual tragic hero of Renaissance drama, including Shakespeare's own Othello and Macbeth. Hamlet does not move from a state of well-being or happiness to adversity and suffering. Nor is his state of unhappiness attributed to the death of a beloved and honored father; rather, it is the marriage of his mother to his uncle, who now is King of Denmark. This is implicit in his first words, an aside. When Claudius refers to him as cousin and son, the Prince remarks bitterly: "A little more than kin, and less than kind" (65). He is saying that the uncle-father relationship is monstrous in the literal sense, that is, contrary to the law of nature.

Hamlet's next words are addressed to Claudius and heard by others. They include a quibble. Do the clouds of grief still hang on him? No, he is "too much i' th' sun" (67). Clearly, this young Prince and university student has a gift for irony, one which presupposes intellectuality and involves a kind of grim humor. At the literal level he is saying that he is sunburnt; at the metaphorical level he is saying that, having lost first a father and then a mother, he is unsheltered. It is quite possible, as some have suggested, that Hamlet also puns upon the word *sun*, since the sun was often used as a symbol of kingship and the word, of course, is a homonym of *son*. Obviously Hamlet deeply resents Claudius' referring to him as his son. It should be added that those who see *Hamlet* primarily as an ambition play find here their first evidence that the tragic hero is motivated by a strong desire to dethrone Claudius and to rule Denmark.

Much critical attention has been directed to Hamlet's emphatic use of the word *seems* when his mother asks him, "Why seems it [his father's death] so particular with thee?" (75), and to his use of the expression "*shows* of grief . . . that a man might *play*." His own feeling "passeth *show*." It has been argued that here Shakespeare develops the theme of appearance versus reality and that he intends to stress Hamlet's dedication to truth in contrast to appearances which serve others, notably Claudius. Certainly he is presented as a discordant figure in this assembly, and his "inky cloak" and suit of "solemn black" provide a telling criticism of Claudius and Gertrude. Others may act a part, making use of "windy suspiration of forc'd breath" (sighing) and "fruitful river in the eye" (weeping); Hamlet is incapable of such posturing.

As has been stated above, the overwhelming cause of Hamlet's grief is revealed in his soliloquy: the incestuous union of his mother and his uncle. Since the doctrine involved here is not a current one, and indeed was not universal when Shakespeare wrote *Hamlet*, some explication is desirable. That marriage between a man and his dead brother's wife not only took place but also was sometimes legally authorized before and after Shakespeare wrote the play is undeniable. But according to the canonical law which informs Shakespeare's play, such a marriage is strictly forbidden. That law is based upon the sacramental view of a mystical bond formed in marriage which creates a relationship between man and wife as close as that which exists between blood relations. From the religious point of view, which cannot be ignored if one is to do justice to Shakespeare's intentions, the marriage of Claudius and Gertrude is, to use the official language of the period, "incestuous and unlawful and altogether null and void." To be sure, one wonders why the subjects of the King and Queen voiced no protest or expressed no feeling of shock. But for the poet-dramatist's purpose, it is enough that the young, idealistic Christian Prince should believe that the honor of the Danish royal family has been stained. It may be added that, traditionally, incest was considered to be an offense against the whole of society. If that view is applicable in Shakespeare's play, then Hamlet has a public duty to oppose Claudius, and the issue is not merely a personal, or domestic, one.

So great is Hamlet's grief that, were it not for the religious injunction against suicide, that ultimate act of despair and thus a mortal sin, he would take his own life: "O, that this too too solid flesh would melt. . . . " Since the Second Quarto has *sallied* for *solid*, some editors and critics are convinced that Hamlet actually speaks of his "sullied" flesh, a reading that certainly illuminates the Prince's attitude toward the marriage. Here, then, is the crushing discovery of great evil by a young idealist. Little wonder that his world has become "stale, flat, and unprofitable." The metaphor Hamlet uses is fitting: his world has become an "unweeded garden." Elsewhere in Shakespeare's plays, notably in *Richard II*, garden and weed imagery is used for the development of theme. The properly tended garden represents an orderly world; weeds represent disease or corruption which destroys order.

Consistent with this outlook, Hamlet identifies his dead father with Hyperion in comparison to Claudius, who is likened to a satyr. Hyperion, or Apollo, was the god of light, and light traditionally has been equated with order and virtue. A satyr is something of a goatish caricature of a human being, and has attained the secondary meaning of "lecherous man." For Hamlet, lust, not love, determines the relationship between Claudius and Gertrude. According to the moral philosophy of the Renaissance, lust was viewed as evidence of general degradation, involving bestiality and the rejection of God-given reason. The Prince now sees his mother as incapable of love, for he refers to her earlier regard for King Hamlet in terms of physical appetite:

> Why, she would hang on him
> As if increase of appetite had grown
> By what it fed on. . . .

(143-45)

Most devastating is his indictment:

> O, most wicked speed, to post
> With such dexterity to incestuous sheets!

(156-57)

In this soliloquy, Hamlet first demonstrates his considerable ability to move from particulars to generalization. If a mother and wife who appeared so loving can so degrade herself, then all women, all daughters of Eve, are immoral: "Frailty, thy name is woman!" (146). It will be, perhaps, to test his own conclusion that Hamlet will turn to Ophelia— so some competent critics have reasoned.

Facing this tormenting situation, Hamlet says that he "must hold [his] tongue" (159)—that is, he can do nothing. But perhaps some indication that he is called upon to act has been provided. Claudius, he declares, is no more like his royal brother than Hamlet himself is to Hercules (152-53). The Prince's disparagement of his own prowess may suggest that, heretofore uncalled upon to prove himself, he soon will face a task which, in its way, will be as challenging as any of the labors of Hercules.

"I am glad to see you well," says Hamlet perfunctorily when Horatio greets him, interrupting his thoughts. But then he is all graciousness and warmth when he recognizes his friend and fellow-student.

Some have seen all this either as a sudden change in mood (which is an early indication of emotional instability caused by excessive grief) or merely as an effort on Hamlet's part to control himself. But it may be more reasonable to conclude that, for the first of many times in this play, Shakespeare provides a glimpse of Hamlet's normal self—the Hamlet before his tragedy began, as it were.

The mention of the funeral provokes Hamlet's grimly witty replies. Surely Horatio has returned to attend the wedding of Hamlet's mother for which "The funeral bak'd-meats/Did coldly furnish forth the marriage tables" (180-81). However high-spirited, these words reveal that his mood has changed back to that of profound melancholy. Quite naturally he evokes mentally the image of his father, and quite naturally Horatio is startled. The transition to Horatio's report of what he and the guard have seen is thus skillfully achieved. Before proceeding, however, one should not ignore Hamlet's tribute to his father. In the soliloquy, the late king was identified with a Greek god; here Hamlet does not depend upon the language of the scholar and, if anything, pays greater homage: "He was a man, take him for all in all, I shall not look upon his like again" (187-88). A *man*, a *human* being, not "a beast, that wants discourse of reason." In both *King Lear* and *Macbeth*, two of the four great Shakespearean tragedies which include *Hamlet*, the dramatist uses the word *man* in this sense. The implications with reference to Claudius, who now rules Denmark and calls himself Hamlet's father, are evident.

It is an excited Prince who cross-examines Horatio, Marcellus, and Bernardo: "Where was this? . . . Did you not speak to it? . . . Arm'd, say you? . . . Stay'd it long?" There follows the expression of determination to "watch to-night" and his insistence that they tell no one else what they have seen. Perhaps there is significance in Hamlet's question, "Then saw you not his [not *its*] face?" (228). At this point, the question may indicate that the Prince is sure that the Ghost is "honest," not a "goblin damn'd"; later he will not be so sure. To be noted also is the fact that Horatio reports that the Ghost appeared "more/In sorrow" than in anger, a statement that is contrary to his earlier observation.

The words that Hamlet speaks alone at the end of this scene suggest, first, that he now considers the possibility of the apparition's being an omen of evil; and, second, that he suspects some "foul play."

ACT I – SCENE 3

Summary

In a room at Polonius' house, Laertes is saying farewell to Ophelia, his sister. Assuming the perogatives of a brother, he has words of advice for her. She is not to take seriously Hamlet's attentions and, above all, must be wary to protect her virtue. Ophelia goodnaturedly accepts this advice but urges her brother to practice what he preaches.

Polonius enters, telling his son not to delay and then offering him fatherly advice on how to conduct himself. Laertes departs, and Polonius turns to his daughter to find out what her brother has been saying to her. When Ophelia replies that it related to Hamlet, who has "of late made many tenders/Of his affection" for her, the elderly father remarks that he has heard that the Prince has been attentive to her. He scoffs at the very thought that Hamlet's intentions are serious and honorable, and he warns her to conduct herself so as not to make him appear a fool. He knows how young men importune young ladies and for what purpose. Ophelia is to avoid the Prince's company. "I shall obey," replies this dutiful daughter of the Lord Chamberlain.

Commentary

In this scene one meets Polonius and his family at home and learns much about each member, particularly the son and the father. Moreover, a new story element is introduced — Hamlet's apparent love for Ophelia.

How does Laertes appear? On the debit side, he seems to be the devoted brother quite rightly concerned with protecting his young sister; he also seems to be the dutiful son who accords his father proper respect. But in the total of fifty-three lines of blank verse which constitute Laertes' lecture on sisterly conduct, the note of artificiality and lack of spontaneity come through strongly. This is the contrived style of the young courtier, with a succession of metaphors, studied parallelisms, and antitheses. Taken together with Polonius' advice to his son and his words to his daughter, Laertes' lines suggest a limitation as regards the family's concept of honor.

Polonius' lines are even more revealing. His advice to Laertes (59-80) comprises one of the very well-known passages in the play. Although some early commentators took the Lord Chamberlain's words to be "golden" and as evidence of profound wisdom, the consensus is that the elderly Lord Chamberlain is merely parroting copybook maxims familiar to any Elizabethan schoolboy. His lines reveal a vain and limited character. As one informed critic has pointed out, most of what Polonius tells his son relates to etiquette, not ethics (H. Levin, p. 25). This father is coaching his son on how to "act," how to "seem," how to "show" himself publicly. Yet his final precept is ethical, not practical, worldly counsel:

> This above all: to thine own self be true,
> And it must follow, as the night the day,
> Thou canst not then be false to any man.
>
> (77-79)

Climaxing his rather long speech, this change of tone can only be taken ironically.

If all this seems to be unduly harsh at this early stage of the action, consider his questions and remarks to Ophelia, who dutifully reports that Hamlet has "made many tenders/Of affection" but has done so "In honourable fashion." Polonius flatly rejects the possibility of sincere affection; he is convinced that "the holy vows of heaven" are no more than snares to entrap the innocent and unwary. He seems to take positive delight in his own off-color interpretation of Hamlet's recent interest in his daughter. Most damaging is his admonition:

> Tender yourself more dearly,
> Or—not to crack the wind of the poor phrase,
> Running it thus—you'll tender me a fool.
>
> (107-9)

Vanity and suspicion come through strongly in this passage. Polonius appears to be much more concerned about his public image than about the welfare of his daughter. And his emphasis is also upon how one should play a role, how one should act, show, seem.

One other significant point is made clear in this scene, one relating to the status of Hamlet. He is not a *private* individual but a *public* one; what he does has public, not merely personal, import. This Laertes says:

> His greatness weigh'd, his will is not his own;
> For he himself is subject to his birth.
> He may not, as unvalued persons do,
> Carve for himself, for on his choice depends
> The sanity and health of the whole state. . . .
>
> (17-21)

This is the first passage which has been cited to support the argument that Hamlet unmistakably has the duty to avenge his father's death and to do so without procrastination.

ACT I—SCENE 4

Summary

Near midnight Horatio and Marcellus again appear on the platform before the castle. As pre-arranged, Hamlet is now with them. When cannon fire and the sound of trumpets are heard, the Prince explains that the King and members of his court are participating in a revel during which the wine flows freely and "the swagg'ring up-spring reels"— that is, all are participating in boisterous dancing. Hamlet tells Horatio that such drunken revelry has earned for the Danes a reputation for drunkenness. This leads him to reflect aloud on how one particular fault may lead to "general censure."

"Look, my lord, it comes!" exclaims Horatio. The Ghost has made its appearance. Whether it comes from heaven or hell, Hamlet declares that he will address it and call it "Hamlet, King, father." He implores the Ghost to answer him, but instead it beckons to the Prince. Horatio urges Hamlet not to follow the Ghost, warning him that it may lead him to his death. Both Marcellus and Horatio forcibly try to hold back the Prince, but he will not be restrained. He threatens to make a ghost of the one who tries to stop him and orders both to stand apart. Convinced that Hamlet is in a state of desperation, the two decide to follow the Prince and the Ghost.

Commentary

Once more, setting and mood are provided economically in broken lines of blank verse and informal diction. It is very close to midnight, the hour when the spirit appeared on the previous occasion.

Hamlet's "dram of evil" speech (19-38) is of special interest and possibly of major importance. Inspired as it is by his reaction to the sound of drunken revelry coming from the court where Claudius fulfills his pledge to celebrate what he called Hamlet's "gentle and unforc'd accord" (I.ii.123-28), the Prince again demonstrates his ability to move from particulars to generalization. Propensity for excessive drink, encouraged now by the King himself, leads other nations to use the "swinish phrase" *drunkards* when speaking of the Danes; in the same way, a fault in an individual may override his virtues and lead to his downfall.

Many commentators argue, understandably, that the subject of Hamlet's discourse is specifically the reputation of Claudius, who now rules Denmark but who, according to Hamlet, is no more like his predecessor than is Hyperion to a satyr. The King's taking "his rouse" may also serve to illustrate the deterioration of Elsinore since the death of King Hamlet. Moreover, his speech may be intended to illustrate the Prince's propensity for thought; those who accept the Romantic view of a Hamlet rendered incapable of positive action by this very propensity find no reason for looking for more in the "dram of evil" speech.

But, as has been stated in the introduction to these Notes, a sufficient number of distinguished Shakespeareans consider Hamlet to be a superior individual who, nevertheless, becomes a slave of passion. To them, these lines incorporate an exploration of the problem of good and evil (the problem basic to tragedy) and may well provide the key to the Hamlet mystery. Their views deserve notice.

When one hears Hamlet speak of the "o'ergrowth of some complexion," "the stamp of one defect," corruption from a "particular fault" leading to the corruption of an individual "as pure as grace" in other ways, the inclination is to believe that Shakespeare is underscoring a significant theme. Hamlet provides three possible answers to the problem of evil — three reasons why there may be present "some vicious mole of nature" which may lead to general censure and downfall. The first one is inherited defect ("As, in their birth"), which obviously does not involve human responsibility, the individual being a victim of fate ("fortune's star"). If that were the answer in *Hamlet*, then the play cannot be classified as Renaissance high tragedy, but rather as one based on, or consistent with, the Medieval theory, according to which individual choice and responsibility have no place.

The second answer involves the "o'ergrowth of some complexion" which often breaks "down the pales and forts of reason." Here human responsibility is evident. Some knowledge of Renaissance moral theory relating to the "complexions" is required if one is to understand Hamlet's words. At the simplest literal level, the term *complexion* may be defined as "natural quality." But for Shakespeare's generation, it had a more specific meaning. It referred to a person's temperament resulting from the supposed combination of four bodily fluids called "humours." The complexions were sanguine, melancholic, choleric, and phlegmatic. Proper balance of the humours in the body made possible the healthy individual; an excess or deficiency of one humour led to a psychological or physical imbalance. According to this theory, so widely accepted in the Elizabethan and Jacobean ages, the intellectual was especially susceptible to melancholy, often in its extreme form, which was called melancholy adust. This passion of excessive grief negated the powers of reason and thus the ability to act positively. Those who see Hamlet as the victim of excessive grief which causes him to delay or to act only on impulse find here support for this theory. That the Prince himself should provide doctrinal support, it is argued, is not surprising: his intellectual superiority is well established in the play and, in the course of the action, he emerges as the best critic of himself on more than one occasion.

The third answer is that relating to "some habit that too much o'erleavens [mixes with]/The form of plausive [pleasing] manners." Excessive drink obviously is one such habit, and it is the one which Hamlet must have in mind, in view of the carousal which motivates his speech. Such a habit, like the "o'ergrowth of some complexion," may lead an individual, however virtuous he may appear to be in other respects, to reject reason, the quality which distinguishes him from the beast. It will be recalled that Hamlet uses bestial imagery in referring to the drunken revelry, speaking of how the "kettle-drum and trumpet thus bray out" (11) and of the "swinish phrase" used to describe those prone to excessive drinking. Obviously, the charge of bestiality could be applicable only to Claudius. But Hamlet himself is deeply concerned with public reputation and certainly with the honor of his family. One need not fear that he will be guilty of indulging a bad habit leading to the rejection of reason. If any of the answers to the problem of evil which he advances turn out to be applicable to him, it must be either adverse fate or uncontrolled passion.

"Angels and ministers of grace defend us!" exclaims Hamlet as he sees the apparition for the first time, voicing the orthodox Christian formula to be used on such a terrifying occasion. Consistent with contemporary ideas relating to ghosts, he knows that it may be "a spirit of health" (one divinely allowed to return to accomplish a rightful mission) or a "goblin damn'd" (an evil spirit, a devil, or even the Devil himself) appearing in the form and dress of King Hamlet and intent on leading the Prince to destruction—perhaps to draw him into madness, as Horatio warns (69-78). But, in the stress of powerful emotion, Hamlet makes a positive identification of the Ghost as "King, father; royal Dane" (45). He assumes that the spirit has come from the grave where the body of King Hamlet, in "the very armour he had on/When he th' ambitious Norway combated" (I.i.60-62), had been buried.

Despite argument and attempts to restrain him physically, the Prince obeys the summons of the Ghost. What if his life be threatened? Having listened to him voice his innermost thoughts, one knows that he does not value life in a world where traditional virtues no longer flourish.

ACT I—SCENE 5

Summary

The Ghost tells Hamlet that it is the spirit of his father, doomed for a time to walk on earth during the nights and to endure purgatorial fires during daytime in expiation for sins committed during life. The Ghost calls upon him to prove his love for his father: "Revenge his foul and most unnatural murder." Hamlet is told that although King Hamlet's death was attributed to the sting of a serpent, it was Claudius, "that incestuous, that adulterate beast," who murdered his brother. The Prince receives this startling news as if it were confirmation of his suspicions. The Ghost then fills in the details. The lustful Claudius, who won the affections of Queen Gertrude, poured poison into the ear of the sleeping King Hamlet, sending him to his death without sacraments and Extreme Unction, thus depriving him at once "Of life, of crown, and queen." No longer must Denmark be ruled by the incestuous murderer; Hamlet is called upon to kill his uncle. But the Ghost adds a word of caution: the son is not to contaminate himself by seeking to punish his mother; he is to leave her punishment to heaven and to her own conscience. "Hamlet, remember me," the Ghost intones as it departs. The Prince solemnly vows to wipe away all else from his memory except that which the Ghost has told him.

It is a highly excited Hamlet who answers the calls of Horatio and Marcellus. His replies to their questions are evasive. When he calls upon the two to take an oath of secrecy regarding what they have seen this night, the voice of the Ghost is heard repeatedly from below the platform: "Swear." Hamlet moves wildly about the platform, now addressing the Ghost, now calling upon his friends to place their hands upon his sword and take the oath. In a more restrained mood, the Prince enlarges the conditions of the oath. If he chooses to pretend to be mentally deranged, they are not to give the slightest indication that they know the reason for his behavior. Again the Ghost's voice is heard: "Swear." When the oath is taken, Hamlet, now subdued, thanks his friends and then expresses his heartfelt desolation.

Commentary

One of the prime concerns of the Ghost is that, as a mortal, it was denied the opportunity to be shriven (receive absolution for sins prior to death) and thus must endure spiritual purgation before it can be admitted to heaven. But what of the "foul crimes" admitted to have been committed by King Hamlet, the man whom his son so much reveres? Obviously he was not perfect; no mortal is, according to church doctrine because mankind remains tainted as the result of original sin. The Ghost is only too aware of mortal imperfections; it has a conscience practically Calvinistic in its strictness.

Hamlet will later have doubts about the nature of the Ghost, although they will be dispelled. But some Shakespearean commentators have remained dubious that Hamlet's doubts have been dispelled, and their view should not be ignored. It has been pointed out that a repentant spirit from purgatory would not appear as an armed warrior even if its mortal body had been so accoutred for burial. But since the Ghost's mission is to call upon Hamlet to attack Claudius, who now rules an armed Denmark, its martial costume is held to be the proper one. One may add that it is most effective theatrically.

Nevertheless, a degree of uncertainty remains. When the Ghost warns Hamlet against failure to execute revenge, it employs a simile which is rather strained, especially for a Christian spirit from purgatory, not from the pagan underworld or Elysium:

> And duller shouldst thou be than the fat weed
> That rots itself in ease on Lethe wharf,
> Wouldst thou not stir in this.
>
> (32-34)

Lethe, it will be recalled, is the Greek mythological river of Hades whose waters, when drunk, caused forgetfulness of the past. To be sure, much Renaissance poetry is filled with a mixture of pagan and Christian elements. Yet one recalls that the Ghost "started like a guilty thing" when the cock crew at daybreak (I.ii.148 ff.). Is this the reaction of a Christian spirit? But it must be conceded that in the present scene the Ghost's behavior never suggests guilt. To Hamlet it says, "But soft! methinks I scent the morning's air./Brief let me be" (58-59). In the earlier scene, dawn began to break before the Ghost, unable to speak its words to the proper person, was aware that its allotted time was up. When Horatio reported what he had seen, he said only that "it shrunk in haste" away (I.ii.219). His earlier words were natural enough under the circumstances; they emphasized his uncertainty and fright.

The climax of the Ghost's recital is reached after just twenty-two lines:

> If thou didst ever thy dear father love—
> . . . .
> Revenge his foul and most unnatural murder.
>
> (23/25)

The two major issues basic to Hamlet's tragedy are now joined: the murder of a king and father, and the marriage of Claudius and Gertrude. The slaying of a king especially is foul and unnatural because he is God's minister on earth, so loyal Elizabethans and Jacobeans fervently believed. The Ghost denounces Claudius as "that incestuous, that adulterate beast" (41) and speaks of Gertrude as that "seeming-virtuous queen" (46). Hamlet is implored not to let "the royal bed of Denmark be/A couch for luxury [sensuality] and damned incest" (82-83). The adultery and incest, which concern the Ghost quite as much as does the murder by means of "leperous distilment," may simply refer to the marriage. Whether or not Gertrude was unfaithful prior to the death of King Hamlet remains a disputed point. But one thing is clear: Prince Hamlet is not alone in his revulsion, unless this Ghost is indeed a "goblin damn'd," intent upon leading the young Prince to destruction—or unless one takes the unusual and radical view that Hamlet, separated from his companions on the platform, is the victim of a hallucination and that the Ghost is actually voicing Hamlet's own thoughts. If this is indeed "an honest Ghost," its concern for the purity of "the royal bed of Denmark," as well as the Crown, suggests that Hamlet is being called upon to execute public justice, not private revenge. Yet this spirit remains curiously tender in its attitude toward Gertrude:

> Taint not thy mind, nor let thy soul contrive
> Against thy mother aught. Leave her to heaven. . . .
>
> (85-86)

The question of the nature of the Ghost and the propriety of its injunction have not yet been answered definitively.

In a state of great excitement, Hamlet declares himself ready to sweep to revenge. He does so even before the identification of the murderer is made and the details of the crime are provided (29-31), although it is reasonable to conclude that he could suspect no one but Claudius. The figurative language which he uses to emphasize his determination deserves attention. He will sweep to his revenge "with wings as swift/As meditation or the thoughts of love" (29-30). The simile is appropriate for a young university scholar and a lover, and Hamlet has been established as both. But does prompt execution of an action involve meditation? In the present circumstances, does it not call for unquestioned, dutiful acceptance of the execution of blood-revenge, an eye for an eye, a tooth for a tooth? Blood-revenge is based on the barbarous *lex talionis,* the primitive law of the blood feud, whereby the nearest of kin is bound to avenge the victim by slaying his murderer. Is Shakespeare, then, restricted by his source or sources, including the original thirteenth-century version by Saxo Grammaticus? Or has he intentionally complicated Hamlet's problem in his play for which he provided a Christian framework?

The Ghost's injunction, "remember me," spoken just before its exit becomes for Hamlet an obsession. From the cellarage, the Ghost repeats the command to "Swear" after Horatio and Marcellus rejoin the distracted Prince. Emotionally, most audiences and readers accept the Ghost as "a spirit of health," just as Hamlet does in this scene. But, if only in afterthought, it remains a puzzling, disturbing thing. It may be relevant, in this connection, that the cellarage (which term gives this scene its usual name) was the cavernous area under the Elizabethan stage which was popularly called "hell."

"Come on; you hear this fellow in the cellarage," says Hamlet to Horatio and Marcellus (151). A few critics wonder if the two friends did hear the Ghost, although Horatio immediately replies, "Propose the oath, my lord." Although he comes close to revealing the Ghost's testimony to his friends, Hamlet does not do so. Both Horatio and Marcellus prove their loyalty to him by taking the solemn oath not to reveal what they have *seen.*

Much has been written about Hamlet's decision to feign madness, "To put an antic disposition on." Some commentators are content to observe that the hero's pose of madness is basic to the original story of Hamlet and must have been included in the pre-Shakespearean *Ur-Hamlet,* and to conclude that audiences expected the hero to feign madness. But such an answer does not suffice for those who refuse to believe that the poet-dramatist permitted himself to be rigidly bound by his source or that he pandered to popular taste in this play, one of his great tragedies. The sources of *Othello* and *Lear* are known and available; his use of those sources establishes his essential independence and originality. Perhaps Hamlet's own words and behavior, after he was joined by his friends, suggested to him the adoption of the antic disposition; clearly he knew that the shock of discovery made impossible normal behavior.

> The time is out of joint; – O cursed spite,
> That ever I was born to set it right.

(189-90)

For Goethe, who envisioned Hamlet as a delicate soul unequal to the performance of the great task laid upon him, these two lines proved the "key to Hamlet's whole procedure" *(Wilhelm Meister,* 1778). Later critics, most of whom do not accept the Romantic interpretation of the Prince's character, nevertheless agree that these are indeed key lines. The Ghost warns Hamlet not to taint his mind by seeking to punish Gertrude. Can he, however, kill his uncle-king without his mind becoming tainted?

ACT II – SCENE 1

Summary

At his home, Polonius instructs Reynaldo to journey to Paris and to give Laertes money and messages. Reynaldo is also given detailed instructions on how to find out if Laertes is conducting himself. Reynaldo is to seek out other Danes in Paris, ones who are sure to know Laertes, and to obtain all the gossip relating to him.

Ophelia enters in a state of fright. She tells Polonius that Hamlet has come to her, his clothes in disarray, his face devoid of color, the very picture of despair. Her father promptly diagnoses Hamlet's condition: the Prince suffers from love-madness brought on by Ophelia's refusal to accept his attention in accordance with her father's instructions. Polonius now believes that he should not have been so strict in this affair. He will inform the King what he has just learned.

Commentary

The late T. S. Eliot found nothing relevant in this scene as far as the instructions to Reynaldo are concerned. Others have argued that it is included only to convey the sense of stagnation in Elsinore, for much time has elapsed since Laertes' departure and Hamlet's encounter with the Ghost. Surely there is much more to be said in justification of this scene.

Earlier the statement was made that this is Hamlet's play and that almost everything any other character says or does relates in some way to him. Polonius is the leading courtier at Elsinore and chief adviser of King Claudius. Already certain limitations in his character have been revealed — the artificiality of his discourse, an inclination toward cynicism and suspicion of other people's motives, and a self-confidence amounting to vanity. This portrait of the Lord Chamberlain, whose major concern earlier was that Ophelia's behavior might tender him a fool, is now no less concerned that Laertes' conduct in Paris does not make him look bad. In his worldliness and cynicism, he is absolutely sure that he knows how young men behave when away from parental control — drinking, fencing, quarreling, and wenching. Reynaldo, Polonius says, is to let Laertes "ply his music" (73); that is, keep a close eye on him and let him reveal his secrets. Not only is Polonius ready to believe the worst about his son, but also he seems to be incapable of honesty in his methods. His outlook and conduct suggest the kind of world in which Hamlet is now living. Indirection — espionage — becomes an elaborate game very soon in this play; this episode prepares the way for it.

The second episode in this scene is concerned with Ophelia's report to her father. From her description of Hamlet, his clothes in disarray, "Pale as his shirt, his knees knocking each other," it is obvious that he has adopted the antic disposition. But when Ophelia says that he appeared

> . . . with a look so piteous in purport
> As if he had been loosed out of hell
> To speak of horrors. . . .
>
> (82-84)

one inevitably recalls the Ghost's revelations. This and other details relating to Hamlet's distress suggest that more is involved here than assumed madness.

Hamlet has chosen to appear before Ophelia, who refused to accept his letters or to let him talk to her, as the courtly lover suffering from amatory ague. It is inconceivable that Hamlet would indulge in such posturing even if Ophelia's rejection of his attentions were a crushing blow. Perhaps, as some critics believe, those "tenders of affection" of which Ophelia spoke earlier may have been made by Hamlet in order to test the validity of his own generalization: "Frailty, thy name is woman!" (I.ii.146). It will be recalled that in the same soliloquy he had declared that all "uses of this world" had become for him "weary, stale, flat, and unprofitable." This hardly suggests that he was in the mood for love. But this is not to deny that Hamlet was attracted to Ophelia. The essential point is this: if one is to do justice to Hamlet's status as a tragic hero who rejects "seeming," it must not be assumed that he now appears as a sentimental poseur. Adopting the antic disposition is something else again. In this world of Elsinore, where Polonius is established as the wisest counselor, the Prince must meet indirection with indirection. Claudius must not learn what Hamlet intends; let his Lord Chamberlain report that his nephew suffers only from love-madness.

Polonius' reaction is, of course, predictable. With complete self-confidence, he declares that Hamlet suffers from "the very ecstasy of love." To be sure, it may be argued that his decision to report to Claudius what he has learned is a proper one under the circumstances, and that he really believes the well-being not only of Hamlet but also of Queen Gertrude to be involved. But when one recalls his prime concern with his own reputation, rather than with the welfare of his daughter, the inclination is to see him as being anxious chiefly to prove how wise he is.

ACT II – SCENE 2

Summary

In the castle, the King, accompanied by his Queen, welcomes Rosencrantz and Guildenstern, who have obeyed his summons to Court. Claudius speaks of Hamlet's strange behavior and asks these two friends of the Prince to see if they can find out the reason. The Queen adds her entreaty that they do so. Showing their respect for royal authority, both agree to do their utmost to learn the cause of Hamlet's affliction. The King and Queen express their gratitude, and the two young men leave.

Polonius enters and announces the return of Cornelius and Voltimand, who were sent as ambassadors to Norway. When Claudius thanks him as "the father of good news," the Lord Chamberlain takes the opportunity to inform the King that he has found the "very cause of Hamlet's lunacy." Claudius urges him to speak of that, but Polonius suggests that the King first receive his ambassadors.

Voltimand is the one who makes the report to Claudius. The elderly and ailing King of Norway has restrained his nephew Fortinbras. Instead of moving against Denmark, the latter agrees to lead his troops against the Poles. The Norwegian ruler asks that Fortinbras be given permission to pass through Danish territory. Claudius expresses his pleasure in hearing the report and states that he will reply to the request after giving it full consideration.

Polonius now holds forth in an elaborate, wordy manner. Hamlet, he declares, is infatuated with Ophelia, in proof whereof the Lord Chamberlain reads a love letter written by the Prince partly in overwrought, highly artificial prose, partly in rhymed lines which never approach poetry. He then provides details relating to Hamlet and Ophelia and concludes that he has indeed found the source and cause of the Prince's affliction. After all, has he ever been found in error when the King has asked him to express his firm opinion? Both Claudius and Gertrude agree that love-madness may indeed explain Hamlet's behavior, but the cautious King wants additional proof. Polonius is ready with a plan. He will let Ophelia meet the Prince; the King and Polonius will conceal themselves and observe the encounter. At the Lord Chamberlain's request, the royal couple and their attendants leave just after Hamlet enters, reading a book, thus giving Polonius a chance to find out what he can from the young Prince.

In his answers to Polonius' questions, Hamlet convinces Polonius that he is indeed the victim of unrequited love. Actually his own questions and his responses comprise scathing ridicule of Polonius. Furthermore, he tacitly warns the Lord Chamberlain that Ophelia's virtue is in jeopardy, and he expresses his own wish for death. Still convinced that he has diagnosed Hamlet's condition accurately, Polonius nevertheless is impressed by what he calls "method" (basic sense) in the Prince's discourse.

When Polonius leaves, Rosencrantz and Guildenstern enter. Hamlet greets them cordially as his "excellent good friends." Yet in the verbal exchange which follows, he becomes increasingly sardonic and suspicious of the motives of these two. Finally he succeeds in making them admit that they had been instructed by the King and Queen to seek him out and to observe him carefully. The Prince then tells them what to report to their majesties: he has lost his mirth and foregone most normal activities because the universe, which he believed to be wondrous, now appears to him to be foul; and man, the so-called paragon of the animals, no longer delights him — nor does woman either. The two then remark that, in his present mood, the Prince will not enjoy the performance of the actors who have just arrived in Elsinore. But Hamlet immediately shows his interest, especially in "He that plays the king."

Learning that these are "the tragedians of the city" whose performances have previously pleased him, Hamlet asks why they are traveling. He is told that an acting company of children have engaged in an attack upon the "common plays" and that theatrical performances by the adult companies have been suspended, popular fancy having turned to the child actors. The Prince then tells Rosencrantz and Guildenstern that they, like the actors, are welcome; but he adds that Claudius and Gertrude are deceived about his madness.

Polonius returns to announce the arrival of the players. Hamlet promptly resumes the antic pose, baiting the elderly Lord Chamberlain but hardly repressing his verbosity. Then, when four or five players enter, he greets them warmly and shows a keen interest in, and knowledge of, the theater.

At Hamlet's request, the First Player recites a set speech from a play based on Aeneas' tale to Dido as told in Virgil's *Aeneid,* one which Hamlet describes as excellent but lacking popular appeal. The speech, which is in epic style, tells of the slaying of King Priam by Pyhrrus, son of Achilles.

After requesting Polonius to see to it that the players are well housed, Hamlet speaks in private to the First Player. It is arranged that on the next day the acting company will present a play called *The Murder of Gonzago,* the script of which will include some twelve to sixteen lines provided by the Prince.

Alone, Hamlet again voices his innermost thoughts. First, he expresses wonder that a player could so realistically portray grief over the death of a character in dramatic fiction. He himself has genuine cause for passion, yet what has he done? Bitterly he denounces himself for failing to act positively against Claudius; he accuses himself of lethargy, cowardice, even villainy. Suddenly the Prince interrupts himself and acknowledges that he has been indulging in futile railing. He then reveals his intentions in having the players enact *The Murder of Gonzago* before the King and the assembled Court. During the performance he will keep his eyes fast on Claudius who, if guilty, will surely flinch and thus inadvertently prove that the Ghost spoke true words. However convinced he had been that it was an "honest" spirit when he listened to its words, Hamlet now is not sure; perhaps it is the Devil who has used his power "to assume a pleasing shape" in order to lead the Prince to damnation.

Commentary

On the surface, Claudius appears gracious, genuinely solicitous about his nephew's well-being, and competent as a ruler in his attention to state affairs. No one should underestimate his capabilities, and these include positive action. Threats against the Crown coming from abroad can be and are met; Cornelius and Voltimand report that Fortinbras will not invade Denmark. But the threat to Claudius implicit in Hamlet's behavior remains. The intensity of the King's concern is evident especially when the confident Polonius assures him that he has "found/The very cause of Hamlet's lunacy." He exclaims, "O, speak of that; that I do long to hear (50)." Gertrude is sufficiently concerned; but it is Claudius, not she, who speaks of Hamlet's madness. Only at Polonius' urging does the King agree to see his ambassadors before exploring that subject. It will be noted that the Queen is not convinced that her son suffers from love-madness:

> I doubt it is no other but the main,
> His father's death and our o'erhasty marriage.
> (56-57)

When Claudius tells Rosencrantz and Guildenstern about Hamlet's "transformation," he says that neither "th' exterior nor the inward man/Resembles that it was" (6-7). Recalling the unctuousness in Claudius' first speech in this play, one may find evidence of Machiavellianism here. Claudius is quite aware of how appearances may deceive—how it is possible to seem, to act a part.

If this generalization on the basis of one brief passage seems to be unwarranted, consider how readily Claudius approves of Polonius' underhanded methods and remains undisturbed by the unsavory terms in which the Lord Chamberlain speaks of them. Polonius refers to hunting the "trail of policy" (47) and says that he will "loose" Ophelia to Hamlet (162). The Prince, apparently, is the prey of hunters, and poor Ophelia is to be cast in the role of a hound. The King's use of the word *sift* ("Well, we shall sift him" (58) is good Elizabethan English, but its connotation here is as unsavory as are the phrases used by the Lord Chamberlain.

In their interview with the King and Queen, Rosencrantz and Guildenstern present themselves as dutiful subjects of the Crown, willing to serve when called upon. Although their supposed concern for Hamlet's well-being is not expressed until the end of this episode, they also appear to be loyal friends of the Prince. Yet the very way in which their concern is expressed arouses some suspicions: "Heaven make our presence and our practices/Pleasant and helpful to him" (38-39). Perhaps the use of the word *practices* suggests that they are not acting unselfishly and honestly, that they fit very well into this atmosphere of suspicion and underhandedness. Moreover, certain echoes in their words and in the words addressed to them may be revealing. *"Both* your Majesties"* might have commanded rather than requested, says

Rosencrantz (26-29); "we *both* obey," chimes in Guildenstern. The latter goes on to say that they

> give up ourselves, in the full bent
> To lay our services freely at your feet,
> To be commanded.
>
> (30-32)

This is indeed a strained way of saying that they will honor Claudius' request. "Thanks, Rosencrantz and gentle Guildenstern," says the King; "Thanks, Guildenstern and gentle Rosencrantz," echoes the Queen. As one early critic remarked, the parallelism suggests their nullity; it is as if neither were more than half a man.

The return of Cornelius and Voltimand with their report about Fortinbras will have special import much later in the play, but it has some significance here. Among other things, it provides a clear indication of how much time has elapsed since Hamlet saw and listened to the Ghost. Also, here is the third reference to the young Norwegian Prince who, like Hamlet, has lost a father and who, unlike Hamlet, has promptly taken positive action to avenge his father's death. But Fortinbras, one now learns, has mastered passion; he will obey his royal uncle, rejecting the idea of revenge, and will expend his energy in an attack upon Poland. Fortinbras, it would seem, is emerging as a foil to Hamlet, Prince of Denmark.

Matters relating to foreign relations having been settled, Polonius is ready to demonstrate his sagacity in solving the mystery of Hamlet's behavior. Now he emerges as an utter fool — and as a marvelous comic creation — pompous, smug, and frivolous. The Lord Chamberlain's repetitions, parallelisms, play on words — all delivered with supreme confidence in his own ability — result in a full-length picture, perhaps a caricature, of a zany. However exaggerated it may be, Shakespeare prepared his audience for it. Most amusing is the fact that Polonius is his own best critic, as when, after a verbal exercise involving the words *day, night,* and *time,* he concludes:

> Therefore, since brevity is the soul of wit,
> And tediousness the limbs and outward flourishes,
> I will be brief. . . .
>
> (90-92)

And later, despite the Queen's admonition that he provide "more matter, with less art," he indulges in another such exercise involving the words *true* and *pity,* and then concludes: "A foolish figure!" (98).

Such broad comedy is welcome as a relief from tragic seriousness; nevertheless, it is functional in relation to the major action. In Hamlet's world, Polonius is accepted as the wise, if not wisest, counselor; and

Polonius plays that role with all the artifice peculiar to his limited character. Respect for age had an important place in ideal Renaissance philosophy, but it did not follow that an individual who had reached, or was close to, dotage would be permitted to remain in a public position. It must be assumed that earlier, and with strict reference to ordinary affairs, Polonius had proved satisfactory; if this were not so, surely the competent Claudius would not depend upon him to such an extent.

Hamlet's love letter, which Polonius reads, is a curious composition, what with its stilted prose and bad verse. For once, one must agree with Polonius, who immediately sets himself up as a critic of style: " 'beautified' is a vile phrase" (111). It suggests the use of make-up, the "plast'ring art," to use the term Hamlet will employ later. In the first mad scene, Ophelia will enter, asking, "Where is the beauteous majesty of Denmark" (IV.v.21). Her use of another oblique form of the word *beauty* has the same connotation in context as *beautified* does here.

It is generally agreed that the love letter is part of Hamlet's pretense of madness on the grounds that, unless it were contrived, the scholarly Hamlet could never have written it. Certainly it is consistent with the portrait of a lovesick Hamlet, as described by Ophelia, and what has been said with reference to that is applicable here. It seems reasonable to conclude that Hamlet knew that the letter would fall into the hands of the foolish Polonius. Nevertheless, the first two lines of verse may have some special significance:

> Doubt thou the stars are fire,
> Doubt that the sun doth move,

(116-17)

Doubts relating to the stars and sun in the universe arose in the late Renaissance and represented a challenge to the traditional view of the universe. Some find here evidence that Hamlet, after his crushing discovery of great evil, has lost his faith in traditional values, which includes the belief that woman can be both fair and true. Finally, certain Romantics insist that Hamlet suffers primarily because his love for Ophelia has not been requited. Such emphasis on the love theme, however, seriously reduces the element of conflict involving Hamlet and Claudius, and removes the play itself from the realm of high tragedy.

The King and Queen depart with their attendants as soon as they see Hamlet coming. The Queen's words, "But look where sadly the poor wretch comes reading" (168), provide useful stage directions, but they do more. They suggest, as do certain other passages in the play, that Gertrude's love and concern for her son are genuine. The Ghost, commanding Hamlet to "Leave her to heaven," had called her "a weak vessel" – and so she is, for she willingly became a partner in an incestuous marriage. But her ready response to the attentions of Claudius seems to be the extent of her guilt.

Enter Hamlet, reading. This is the Prince who had vowed to "sweep to [his] revenge" without delay, wiping away "all trivial fond records,/ All saws of books" (I.v.31; 99-100). Perhaps through such reading and through contemplation, he has gained emotional control. In this episode his antic disposition, manifested in his satirical baiting of Polonius, actually reveals a rational mind. His replies and questions addressed to the Lord Chamberlain call for rather close attention.

Does Hamlet recognize Polonius? Yes. Polonius is a fishmonger (174), an appellation which the Lord Chamberlain immediately denies. Yet here is Polonius on another fishing expedition using his "bait of falsehood" and, by indirections, seeking to find directions out. Moreover, *fishmonger* was a cant Elizabethan term for *bawd*—not an inappropriate word, however vulgar, for a man who has just declared that he would "loose" his daughter on Hamlet. The Prince may already be aware of the real fisherman, King Claudius, on whose behalf Polonius is acting.

That Hamlet uses a metaphor relating to lust is suggested by his remark "Then I would you were so honest" (176), since the term *honesty* frequently was used as the opposite of *frailty*, or sexual immorality. In so many words, then, Hamlet is denouncing Polonius as being more immoral than a procurer. Apparently the disillusioned idealist, the Prince seems to be obsessed with the subject of honesty. Among those in authoritative positions, he finds no honesty. Even innocent daughters may be corrupted; even the ostensibly healthful rays of the sun may lead to the breeding of maggots in a dead dog, "being a good kissing carrion" (181-82). He does not finish the statement; instead, he suddenly asks Polonius, "Have you a daughter?" Then he provides riddling advice: "Let her not walk i' th' sun. Conception is a blessing, but not as your daughter may conceive" (185-87).

Page after page has been filled with explication of this brief passage with its plays on the words *sun* and *conception*. Among the interpretations widely accepted is that these lines emphasize (1) Hamlet's awareness of rottenness in the Court, and (2) his conviction that Claudius, the new ruler, is the source of that rottenness which threatens to contaminate or destroy all at Elsinore. There remains the possibility that, since Hamlet seems to know that Polonius will "loose" his daughter upon him, Ophelia has become an obsession for Hamlet. The difficulty with this conclusion is that it is exactly the one reached by Polonius. One point is indisputable. Hamlet is overwhelmingly successful in convincing the Lord Chamberlain that he is "far gone," suffering "much extremity for love" (190-92).

That Hamlet the scholar has been preoccupied with the problem of morality is indicated by his reference to "the satirical slave," whose remarks on senility he paraphrases (198-202). The reference is to Juvenal, second-century Roman moral satirist; it follows, then, that the larger subject of Hamlet's discourse in this episode is the prevalence of evil. The Prince's melancholy, never far below the surface, is evident. Once more, death seems to him to be preferable to life. "Will you walk out of the air, my lord?" asks Polonius. "Into my grave?" Hamlet counters (210).

In warmth, Hamlet's greeting of Rosencrantz and Guildenstern as his "excellent good friends" matches the greeting that he accorded Horatio. It at once gives an insight into the normal mood of Hamlet before his tragedy began and reveals his yearning for honest comradeship. Add to this the fact that again he demonstrates his capacity for a quick change of mood. At first his remarks are spontaneous, good-natured ones; but, not long after the subject of Fortune is introduced, they become serious and revealing—specifically when Rosencrantz remarks that he has no news to report "but that the world's grown honest" (241). Rejecting this conclusion, Hamlet, ostensibly changing the subject, speaks of Denmark and the world itself as a prison. From this emerges the theme of ambition. Now Hamlet is fully aware of what these two supposed friends are up to. Characteristically, he asks them in the name of friendship to be honest with him; just as characteristically, they seek to evade a direct answer but are practically forced to admit that the King and Queen have sent for them.

There follows one of the several especially memorable passages in the play, one in which the Prince is revealed as the disillusioned idealist (306-19). Here is a young intellectual who once embraced the Renaissance view of an ordered and moral universe in which man, endowed with reason, was the noblest creature, far above the bestial and near to the angelic. According to this concept, inherited from the Middle Ages, man occupies a place on a hierarchical scale midway between the beast and the angel: the first represents absence or rejection of reason; the second, pure reason which is equated with virtue. But Hamlet has learned that mankind has a terrifying capacity to reject reason, to descend to the bestial level: subjects may murder kings, brother may kill brother; wives and mothers may hasten to incestuous sheets; boyhood friends may permit themselves to be used as spies, rejecting the sacred principles of friendship. Philosophy offers poor consolation under such conditions. For Hamlet, the world has become "a sterile promontory" and man no more than the "quintessence of dust."

Hamlet's speech (304 ff.), which includes the famous apostrophe to man is more than a purple patch; it has significance in terms of the plot.

Hamlet finds it desirable to explain his emotional state to Rosencrantz and Guildenstern, and he does so without revealing its cause. Rosencrantz laughs and makes a facetious remark relating to women, and this provides an easy transition to the next episode in this long scene.

Ultimately the actors will serve the Prince in his first positive move against Claudius — reason enough for the announcement of their arrival and for the talk relating to them. But there are other points to be noticed here. "He that plays the king shall be welcome" (332). This is Hamlet's immediate response to the news; it is clearly a reference to Claudius, whom the Prince holds to be no more than a Player-King, however skillful in acting the part. But is there possible relevance in the rivalry between the Children's Company and the adult companies (343 ff.)? Of course this is a topical allusion to the so-called "war of the theaters" — the rise of the companies of child actors which became serious rivals to the adult companies, including Shakespeare's, at the turn of the century. Having learned the details of this "late innovation," as Rosencrantz calls it, Hamlet moves from the particular to the general. His uncle, an object of ridicule when King Hamlet ruled Denmark, is now revered by the populace. The new popularity of both child actor and uncle-king, whom Hamlet sees as a shadow rather than the substance of royalty, illustrates the fickleness of public taste.

Just before the players appear, Polonius enters, confident that only he can inform Hamlet of their arrival. Again he is the target of Hamlet's biting satire. Most of the Prince's remarks the Lord Chamberlain either does not hear or, at least, understand. Just as he had set himself up as an authority on word choice, so now he presents himself as one on drama (414-21). His catalogue of types of Elizabethan drama, pure and hybrid, provides wonderful comedy, all the more amusing because Polonius remains deadly serious. It also reveals Shakespeare's own familiarity with Elizabethan drama, the classical tragedies of Plautus, the tragedies of Seneca, and (to some extent) dramatic theory. With reference to Polonius, the implication is plain. As his advice to Laertes indicated, he is an educated individual; unfortunately, knowledge does not always lead to wisdom. In Polonius' case, vanity and age have taken their toll. If his methods were not so contemptible, perhaps he would deserve sympathy.

"O Jephthah, judge of Israel, what a treasure hadst thou!" exclaims Hamlet (422), having adopted the antic pose to the bewilderment of the Lord Chamberlain. But to paraphrase Polonius' words (207-8), there is method in his "madness." Jephthah sacrificed a beloved daughter, however unwillingly; in a sense, Polonius is sacrificing his daughter.

Hamlet then greets the players, once more demonstrating a rapid change in mood. His warmth and genuine pleasure are apparent. Here, then, is another glimpse of Hamlet's mood prior to his discovery of appalling evil. This Wittenberg student, devoted to his studies, never-theless enjoyed the theater just as he treasured companionship. His witty, good-natured remarks to the bearded player and to the youth who had played women's roles suggest a Hamlet anything but a dreamer. When he recalls the *Aeneas and Dido* play as one devoid of crowd-pleasing sallets (spicy improprieties) and affectation, the Prince an-ticipates the point he will make later in his advice to the players (III.ii.1-16). He endorses restraint and modesty as opposed to excess.

A grateful Hamlet pays tribute to the acting profession and directs Polonius to see that the players are "well us'd." Having made the ar-rangements for the performance of *The Murder of Gonzago* with the insertion of lines to be provided by him, Hamlet is left alone; again he soliloquizes at length. The Prince now emerges as his own severest critic, denouncing himself as "a dull and muddy-mettled [irresolute] rascal," a dreamer "unpregnant of [unstirred by] my cause." But, rather curiously, it is the actor's description of Hecuba's grief, the histrionic display of sorrow for the death of Priam, that Hamlet most wanted to hear and which leads him to inveigh against himself, insisting that he has greater "motive and the cue for passion" (587). Passionate expres-sion of grief is not positive action; indeed, it inhibits action. One won-ders why the Prince did not dwell upon Pyrrhus' act of vengeance which seems to have unmistakable applicability to Hamlet.

Pyrrhus, enraged by the violent death of his father, Achilles, is de-termined to execute vengeance on King Priam, father of Achilles' slayer. Pyrrhus did delay, but only momentarily:

> for, lo! his sword,
> Which was declining on the milky head
> Of reverend Priam, seem'd i' th' air to stick,
> So, as a painted tyrant, Pyrrhus stood
> And, like a neutral to his will and matter,
> Did nothing.
>
> (499-504)

Hamlet unmistakably sees himself as "a neutral to his will and matter." In the lines spoken by the player, Pyrrhus promptly emerges as the per-fect revenger, the very prototype of the king-killer:

> And never did the Cyclops' hammers fall
> On Mars his armour forg'd for proof eterne
> With less remorse than Pyrrhus' bleeding sword
> Now falls on Priam.
>
> (511-14)

A whole school of critics, beginning with the Romantics, have taken Hamlet's self-criticism as the essential truth: he is the inveterate dreamer; he cannot bring himself to act positively until it is too late to prevent his own downfall. But is one to assume that Hamlet, scholar and son of a father idolized for his superior virtues, would identify himself with the blood-smeared Pyrrhus who made "malicious sport/In mincing with his sword [Priam's] limbs" (536-37)? If the Greek warrior is held to be the model of the dutiful son avenging his father's death, little wonder that Hamlet said, after hearing the Ghost's accusation and injunction, "O cursed spite,/That ever I was born to set it right" (I.v.189-90). Yet so intense are his feelings at this point that Hamlet denounces himself as a coward, apparently for not having acted as promptly as Pyrrhus did. And he reaches the climax of passion as he denounces Claudius and cries out for vengeance:

> Bloody, bawdy villain!
> Remorseless, treacherous, lecherous, kindless
> [unnatural] villain!
> O, vengeance!
>
> (608-10)

But Hamlet masters his fury; he is aware that he has permitted passion, not reason, to dominate him. It is now that he reveals his plan to "catch the conscience of the King" — unmistakably to establish Claudius' guilt.

Little wonder that *The Tragedy of Hamlet* has been referred to sometimes as "The Mystery of Hamlet." In the last scene of Act I, Hamlet vowed to sweep to his revenge; weeks have passed and he has not made even an attempt. Many have argued that the wary Claudius, well protected by his palace guard, has not given the Prince a chance to attack him. But there is another complication. After rejoining Marcellus and Horatio, Hamlet declared, "It is an honest ghost, that let me tell you" (I.v.138). Now, at the end of Act II, he has genuine doubts regarding the nature of the Ghost and feels compelled to confirm its testimony. As in the discovery scene, he may speak of heaven, but the thought of hell persists in his mind (See I.v.92-93 and II.ii.613). So far, only when he was in a state of great excitement marked by "wild and whirling words" has Hamlet had no doubts about the Ghost. Although he becomes quite excited emotionally at the climax of his soliloquy, he controls himself and he immediately plans to verify the Ghost's accusation. The conclusion to be drawn is that when Hamlet is in control of his passion, he recognizes, as Horatio did, that the Ghost may represent evil:

> The spirit that I have seen
> May be the devil; and the devil hath power
> T' assume a pleasing shape. . . .
>
> (627-29)

A sufficient number of honored Shakespearean critics agree that this is a real fear, not an excuse for inaction. But the Gonzago play seems to be designed primarily to force Claudius to reveal his guilt rather than to establish the Ghost's honesty. Does it follow, then, that Hamlet is intent upon making clear to all that he will execute public justice, not carry out barbaric blood-revenge?

Some critics insist that this entire scene serves first of all to emphasize Hamlet's inability to act positively. Does not the Prince refer to his "weakness" and his "melancholy" (630)? And was it not the lines dealing with Hecuba's grief which he was most anxious to hear? As has been stated in the introduction to these Notes, certain distinguished Shakespeareans find Hamlet to be a victim of passion — the passion of excessive grief which was known as melancholy adust. Whether or not one agrees that Hamlet delays fatally because he is the victim of the destructive passion of melancholy, the subject deserves attention. Certainly it would be a mistake to ignore the many textual references, direct and indirect, to melancholy. For the immediate purpose, it must suffice to state that when Hamlet speaks of the world as a prison (249-53), when he declares that he has "foregone all custom of exercise" and that for him the earth seems to be "a sterile promontory" and the air "a foul and pestilent congregation of vapours" (305-15), when he tells Rosencrantz and Guildenstern that he is "but mad north-north-west," and that he knows "a hawk from a handsaw" when "the wind is southerly" (396-97), the ideas and words derive from prevailing Renaissance theories on melancholy. According to the theorists, the melancholy individual was prone to dwelling at inordinate length upon his difficulties, real or imagined; but, so far from remaining lethargic, he often would become hysterical and would act impulsively. It must be admitted that much of this could be considered applicable to Hamlet. But, of course, one's sympathies remain with him. He indeed has "great cause" — the moral "falling off" of a mother; the death of a beloved father and king; the survival and elevation to kingship of a man who, however adroit, is manifestly inferior to the late King Hamlet. Moreover, consistent with his honesty with himself and his superior intelligence, the Prince anticipates, as it were, any and all his critics in his recognition that passion threatens to engulf him and to make it impossible for him to be "express [exact] and admirable in action" and "noble in reason."

It is a completely controlled, rational Hamlet who speaks the lines at the very end of this long, complex scene:

> I'll have grounds
> More relative than this. The play's the thing
> Wherein I'll catch the conscience of the King.
> (632-34)

Some stage Hamlets—the late John Barrymore, for example—rendered these lines as hysterical rant; those who grasped the character and situation accurately—Sir John Gielgud, for example—spoke them with vigor and determination, devoid of all rant.

ACT III—SCENE 1

Summary

Rosencrantz and Guildenstern report to the King and Queen that Hamlet admits feeling "distracted" but will not tell them the cause and keeps himself aloof "with a crafty madness." In reply to Gertrude's question, they report that Hamlet received them graciously and seemed pleased to hear of the players' arrival. Polonius adds that the Prince wants the King and Queen to witness the performance of a play. Claudius expresses his pleasure at hearing that Hamlet shows such an interest and agrees to attend the performance. He then instructs Rosencrantz and Guildenstern to encourage Hamlet's new interest. The two depart.

At the King's request, Gertrude leaves. Now Polonius' plan to have Ophelia meet Hamlet while the King and the Lord Chamberlain secretly observe and listen can be put into effect. Polonius instructs his daughter: Ophelia is to appear to be reading a book of devotions so that the Prince will not suspect her purpose. In an aside, Claudius reveals the extent to which Polonius' words lash his conscience. Counselor and King withdraw just before Hamlet enters.

For the third time in the play, Hamlet soliloquizes. He now ponders the question of "To be, or not to be" when one is faced with great difficulties and tribulations. At the sight of Ophelia, he is aroused from contemplation. Assuming that she is indeed reading a book of devotions, he urges her to pray for him.

When Ophelia says that she has certain gifts which she has received from him and now wishes to return, he declares that he has given her nothing. To her bewilderment, he proceeds to question her honesty and denies that he ever loved her, whatever he may have said in the past. All men, Hamlet declares, are "arrant knaves"; none should be believed. Therefore, he concludes, she should seek haven in a nunnery. Quite abruptly the Prince asks Ophelia where her father is. She replies that he is at home. Again he returns to the general subject of love, declaring that, should she ever marry, she will "not escape calumny." And again he gives her bitter advice: "Get thee to a nunnery, go." Left to herself, Ophelia expresses her profound sorrow at witnessing what she is convinced is the overthrow of a noble mind which had been the very pattern of virtue and accomplishment.

Promptly, the King and Polonius join Ophelia. Claudius now is convinced that love is not the cause of Hamlet's affliction; rather, that it is "something in his soul/O'er which his melancholy sits on brood" (172-73). No less convinced that Hamlet's behavior constitutes a great threat to him, the King tells Polonius that he has suddenly decided to have Hamlet conducted to England, whose ruler owes tribute to Denmark. Polonius is still convinced that the Prince suffers from love-madness, but he endorses Claudius' decision. He then tells his daughter that she need not say anything since the King and he heard all. The Lord Chamberlain urges that one more attempt be made to ferret out Hamlet's secret: let the Queen talk with her son severely on the subject of his melancholy while Polonius listens from a place of concealment; then, if Hamlet's secret is not exposed, let Claudius send the Prince to England or confine him elsewhere. "It shall be so," says the King. "Madness in great ones must not unwatch'd go" (195-96).

Commentary

It is an increasingly fearful Claudius who appears in this first scene of Act III, although he remains in control of himself. As the conflict between him and Hamlet intensifies, he demonstrates his decisiveness, his capacity for immediate action. His control is especially manifest in his care to keep up the appearance of being unselfishly concerned about his nephew's well-being and in his apparent graciousness with which he agrees promptly to honor Hamlet's request that he and the Queen witness the performance of the play. But the intensity of his concern makes it clear that he recognizes Hamlet's so-called "turbulent . . . lunacy" as a dangerous threat to himself.

Claudius' aside (50-54) explicitly reveals the mind of a man tormented by guilt. In his aside, Claudius applies the words to himself: "How smart a lash that speech doth give my conscience!" He compares his "painted word" — what he says publicly — to the "harlot's cheek, beautied with plast'ring art" (51-53). Since Hamlet also will dwell upon the "plast'ring art" and upon the subject of illicit sex, the King's words suggest that the Prince is not suffering just from sexual nausea caused by his mother's incestuous marriage. Illicit sex or lust, here represented by the harlot, symbolizes pervading evil and man's descent to the bestial level. "O heavy burden!" the King concludes. He has emerged as a human being, however sinful. Shakespeare has provided Claudius' private confession of guilt, but one is not told here what is the crime or crimes.

Needless to say, Claudius remains the powerful adversary. He is Machiavellian not only in his ability to dissemble and his use of underhanded methods, but also in his capacity for prompt action. Rosencrantz and Guildenstern are directed to renew their efforts and Polonius will be given another chance to verify his judgment. But the King stands ready to send Hamlet away—not back to Wittenberg, but to England, where he can be taken care of in one way or another. "Madness in great ones must not unwatch'd go" (196). This line deserves repetition. It reveals at once the King's increasing fear and his care to express himself so that the listener (Polonius here) assumes that only the welfare of the Prince and the State are involved. Moreover, this line serves to remind members of the audience (and readers) that Hamlet is no ordinary individual. In a hierarchical society he is one of the "great ones"—which means that all that affects him has public, not merely private, import.

Both Polonius and Gertrude remain in character. The Lord Chamberlain is the author of what Claudius chooses to call "lawful espials"; it is he who coaches his daughter on how to play her ignoble part; it is he who remains vainly confident that only he is qualified to counsel the King. If Polonius acknowledges blame for using underhanded methods (46-49), he seems to do so only in vanity, welcoming this chance to display himself as a man of wisdom.

As before, Gertrude shows proper motherly concern for an ailing son. In this connection, it will be noted that she is the one who asks if Rosencrantz and Guildenstern have tried to interest Hamlet in some amusement or other (14-15). But also as before, the Queen accepts uncritically whatever Claudius says and willingly accedes to his wishes. She is the dutiful wife, to be sure—but in a marriage that is incestuous.

The "To be, or not be be" soliloquy (56-89) is surely one of the great dramatic monologues in world literature; it is as well known as any passage in the Shakespearean canon and a favorite selection for memorization. The Prince's meditation transcends the personal. Much of what he says is applicable to all mankind, especially when he provides a generalized list of human miseries:

> For who would bear the whips and scorns of time,
> The oppressor's wrong, the proud man's contumely,
> The pangs of dispriz'd love, the law's delay,
> The insolence of office, and the spurns
> That patient merit of the unworthy takes. . . .
>
> (70-74)

The entire speech has been called the "central soliloquy" in the play, coming as it does at the midpoint of the entire action. It poses many critical problems. In view of the often widely disparate interpretations of this soliloquy, it would be naive to ignore the difficulties of interpretation.

In the first place, the soliloquy comes as something of a surprise after the conclusion of Act II, which exhibited Hamlet rational and determined, intent upon carrying out a positive action that, he was sure, would resolve all doubts relating to Claudius. Now he seems to have reverted to the mood of the first soliloquy (I.ii.129-59) — the mood of the Prince who would welcome death, crushed as he was primarily by his mother's marriage to her brother-in-law. There are lines which may support any one of the major interpretations of the play. The Romantics, who see Hamlet as the dreamer, find support when the Prince says:

> And thus the native hue of resolution
> Is sicklied o'er with the pale cast of thought,
> And enterprises of great pith and moment
> With this regard their currents turn awry,
> And lose the name of action.
>
> (84-88)

Those who are convinced that the tragic hero procrastinates because he is suffering from excessive grief find in the soliloquy one of those violent oscillations of mood typical of the extreme melancholic individual, although the subsequent episode involving Ophelia provides a better example. And then there is that considerable group who finds in this soliloquy evidence of Hamlet's moral scrupulousness which makes it impossible for him to abandon the resources of God-given reason and sweep to his revenge in the manner of Pyrrhus. In his restraint they find an intellectual skepticism and honesty with himself that are commendable. For all three groups of theorists, Hamlet's eloquent speech elucidates his expression of despair at the end of Act I, Scene v:

> The time is out of joint; — O cursed spite,
> That ever I was born to set it right.

"To be, or not to be: that is the question." So Hamlet begins his contemplations. In view of his words shortly thereafter, the assumption usually is made that he is asking whether one should choose to live or to die. But immediately after posing the question, the Prince defines two possible courses, neither one of which involves death and certainly not suicide. First, he asks if passive acceptance of "outrageous fortune" is not the nobler course to follow. Stoic philosophy, particularly the Roman Stoicism of Seneca, inculcated such forbearance. According to the dedicated Stoic, pagan and Christian, the final aim of moral action is to destroy passion since no action can be virtuous unless it proceeds from a healthy and upright will.

The second course involves positive action — taking "arms against a sea of troubles,/And by opposing end them." If, as is widely held, Hamlet has a public obligation to remove the rottenness in Denmark, Shakespeare here may have had in mind the contrasting philosophical arguments of Cicero, which vied with those of Seneca in popularity among educated Elizabethans. In his orations, Cicero ridiculed Stoicism, arguing that cloistered virtue is a form of cowardice. On the basis of all this, it follows that Hamlet indeed faces a moral dilemma.

The young Prince next considers a third possible solution to his problem — suicide. Unlike the Greek and certain Roman Stoics, Seneca argued against self-slaughter. One is puzzled because Hamlet expresses thoughts that are completely at variance with those he voiced earlier, and for that matter with what he has experienced. In the first soliloquy, he showed himself to be restrained by his knowledge that "the Everlasting had . . . fix'd/His canon 'gainst self-slaughter" (I.ii.131-32). But the Christian argument finds no place in this later soliloquy. Hamlet states, in effect, that oblivion may be preferable — but only if death brings oblivion:

> To die; to sleep; —
> To sleep? Perchance to dream! Ay, there's the
> rub [obstacle in a game of bowls];
> For in that sleep of death what dreams may come,
> When we have shuffl'd off this mortal coil,
> Must give us pause.
>
> (64-68)

The reason for this fear of death (if that is what it is) is made more explicit in three memorable lines:

> But that the dread of something after death,
> The undiscover'd country from whose bourn
> No traveller returns, puzzles the will. . . .
>
> (78-80)

How are these lines to be interpreted? Does Hamlet not reject the possibility that the Ghost was the spirit of his father? Earlier in the play he spoke of his soul as immortal (I.v.66-67). Why now should it be that the thought of death "puzzles the will"? The Ghost described its condition of afterlife, not as an "undiscover'd country" but as the Catholic purgatory necessary for the soul's purification before translation to heaven. Has Hamlet now embraced the Elizabethan Protestant belief, stated and amplified in sermon and devotional literature that, once separated from the body, the soul cannot return to this world? The eminent Swiss reformer Henry Bullinger (1504-1575), many of whose works were translated into English, wrote on this very subject in words which anticipate those of Shakespeare found in this soliloquy. Souls "go a journey, chancing into unknown countries . . . from whence they cannot return." Perhaps the dramatist has simply made poetic use of what had become a popular tradition by the time he wrote *Hamlet*. There may be another explanation; Shakespeare may have had in mind the difference between the return from the grave of an individual like Lazarus in flesh and blood, in contrast to the return of the spirit, or soul. But one thing is clear. Hamlet has not departed from Christianity; there is no evidence that he doubts the existence of heaven and hell, both of which prompt him to his revenge, or so he has said.

All this does not exhaust the complexities in this soliloquy. Hamlet concludes with these lines:

> Thus conscience does make cowards of us all
> And thus the native hue of resolution
> Is sicklied o'er with the pale cast of thought,
> And enterprises of great pith and moment
> With this regard their currents turn awry,
> And lose the name of action.
>
> (83-88)

Do these lines point unmistakably to a Hamlet who falters after the discovery of great evil and who has difficulty deciding what action can be taken without violating one's own moral code?

Consider the first aphoristic line. In general usage, *conscience* means ethical sense or scrupulousness; its function is to determine the moral quality of action, enjoining what is good. Prompt action without concern for morality is not desirable.

The word *conscience,* however, also meant "consequences" in Shakespeare's time. That meaning is applicable here, since Hamlet has been speaking of suicide as an escape from life's burdens. Understandably, some critics insist that fear of death, even if that death be the result of suicide or not, goes far toward explaining his procrastination. But would one prefer a Hamlet who did not pause to reflect upon the morality involved in "enterprises of great pith and moment"? It has been held that Hamlet's comment "Thus conscience does make cowards of us all" is the central utterance in the play, for it reveals the civilized and Christian Hamlet incapable of revenge (C. B. Purdom, *What Happens in Shakespeare,* London, 1963, p. 83).

The Prince has been restrained by doubts relating to the nature of the Ghost that would have him execute prompt revenge on Claudius but have him leave Gertrude "to heaven." That is indisputable. But there are two other possible reasons for Hamlet's delay. The players have just arrived at Elsinore, and only now does Hamlet have an opportunity to force Claudius into a position where the guilt acknowledged in his private thoughts may be exposed publicly. There is also the possibility that he is held back by his awareness of his intense personal hatred of his uncle-king. Schooled in idealistic philosophy and religious thought, he may believe that his motive for action is not a pure one — that the personal element contaminates that of public justice. If any or all of this be true, then the soliloquy is not to be interpreted as just another manifestation of morbid introspection peculiar to a philosophical dreamer or to an individual suffering from the passion of excessive grief.

The episode which follows provides a shocking change of mood and shows a Hamlet cruel in his treatment of Ophelia.

Shakespeare prepared his audience for this episode which relates back to the one in Act II, Scene ii, where Hamlet baited Polonius with riddling words: "Let her [your daughter] not walk i' th' sun. Conception is a blessing, but not as your daughter may conceive. Friend, look to't" (185-87). Polonius has not looked to it; in the King's service, he has "loosed" Ophelia upon Hamlet. As in the earlier episode, the Prince introduces the theme of honesty—an obsession with him, be it with reference to his own manifestations of grief ("Seems, madam! Nay, it is; I know not 'seems.'"), the nature of the Ghost, the behavior of one-time friends, or the moral character of women. In view of all this, it is difficult to avoid the conclusion that Hamlet, like members of the audience, is fully aware of what is happening: Ophelia is being used just as Rosencrantz and Guildenstern were used; the King and Polonius are spying on him even now. Hamlet, it would appear, is only too aware that Ophelia represents "innocent love" corrupted—coming to him not of her own volition but as a spy seeking by indirections to find directions out. And the ultimate source of the corruption is King Claudius, who rules in a world where women prove "frail" and few men can be believed.

Hamlet's mood is exactly that which dominated him when, after eulogizing man, he said to Rosencrantz and Guildenstern, "Man delights not me,—no, nor woman neither, though by your smiling you seem to say so" (II.ii.321-22). No individual can escape contamination in the world as Hamlet now finds it. Not without logic, then, the disillusioned Prince declares that he had never given Ophelia tokens of love and that he was never honest with her:

> You should not have believ'd me, for virtue cannot
> so innoculate our old stock but we shall relish it.
> I loved you not.
>
> (118-20)

In other words, since the Fall of Adam and Eve, all are sinners, none can escape corruption. Hamlet accuses himself of pride, vengefulness, selfish ambition—indeed of more offenses than he is able to think of: "We are arrant knaves all; believe none of us." These words are heard by Ophelia and overheard by Claudius and Polonius; but Hamlet really speaks to and for Everyman.

What then can Ophelia do? Hamlet tells her: "Go thy ways to a nunnery" (131-32). That he is fully aware that Ophelia has been and remains chaste, that she is the hapless victim of a father incapable of honest methods, is implicit in Hamlet's admonition:

> If thou dost marry, I'll give thee this plague for
> thy dowry: be thou as chaste as ice, as pure as
> snow, thou shalt not escape calumny. Get thee to a
> nunnery, go.
>
> (139-42)

Surely these lines would have little significance if Ophelia were unchaste and if Hamlet were not aware of how she had been "loosed" upon him.

There is a second level of meaning here, one which is consistent with Hamlet's bitter statement that time has proven feminine beauty and honesty to be incompatible (111-16). In the present scene, he says that women make monsters of the men they marry (143-44); and, like the harlots of whom the conscience-stricken Claudius spoke in his aside, their cheeks are "beautied with plast'ring art" and they seek to excuse their wantonness as ignorance (148-52). After this devastating pronouncement, Hamlet repeats the injunction: "To a nunnery, go." In the slang of the militantly Protestant Elizabethan England, the term *nunnery* also meant "brothel." No member of Shakespeare's sixteenth- and seventeenth-century audience was likely to miss this scurrilous second level of meaning.

That the ultimate source of Hamlet's cynicism is his mother's marriage to her brother-in-law is evident when he says: "Those that are married already (all but one) shall live, . . ." (155-56). This includes an unmistakable reference to Claudius and probably a threat. Left to herself, Ophelia speaks lines which at once reveal the genuineness of her lost love and provide a full-length portrait of Hamlet before his tragedy began. It is the picture of the completely accomplished Renaissance man:

> O, what a noble mind is here o'erthrown!
> The courtier's, soldier's, scholar's, eye, tongue, sword;
> The expectancy and rose of the fair state,
> The glass of fashion and the mould of form,
> The observ'd of all observers, quite, quite down!
>
> (158-62)

She is convinced that Hamlet is insane. He is not, however emotionally disturbed he may be. Nevertheless, it is possible that she expresses a basic truth — or so some respected critics believe. Perhaps Hamlet's suffering has resulted in such extreme disillusionment and melancholy that a once noble mind has been overthrown in the sense that he has become passion's slave. Certainly this interpretation is not to be ignored.

Emerging with Polonius from the hiding place, Claudius rejects the theory that his nephew suffers from love-madness, but, like his Lord Chamberlain, he is aware of an apparent method in the Prince's alleged madness. In a state of uncertainty, he will allow Polonius another chance to force Hamlet into revealing the cause of his strange behavior. But if that proves futile, the King will have Hamlet sent to England. It is to be noted that Claudius continues to present the public image of a man who is unselfishly concerned and especially of one dedicated to the welfare of the State. This is implicit in his final line, which also includes an involuntary tribute to Hamlet's status: "Madness in great ones must not unwatch'd go."

ACT III – SCENE 2

Summary

Hamlet instructs the players how to deliver the lines of *The Murder of Gonzago* and discusses the art of acting in general, urging them to avoid unnatural extremes in the imitation of an action. Polonius enters with Rosencrantz and Guildenstern; he announces that the King and the Queen are ready to "hear" the play.

While members of the Court assemble, Hamlet praises Horatio for his steady temperament and then gives him the details relating to *The Murder of Gonzago*. He asks Horatio to keep close watch on the King, just as he himself will do, and to note the King's reaction to one speech in particular. If Claudius does not reveal guilt at that point, the Prince continues, both have seen "a damned ghost," not the honest spirit of the late King Hamlet. The faithful Horatio assures the Prince that he will follow the instructions carefully.

The Court group enters the hall. Claudius greets his nephew and receives a baffling reply. There follows a brief exchange between Hamlet and Polonius. When his mother invites him to sit beside her, Hamlet declines, lying down at Ophelia's feet.

The play itself is preceded by a dumb-show or pantomime, depicting a king and queen deeply in love with each other. When the king falls asleep on a bed of flowers, the queen departs. A man enters, removes the king's crown and kisses it, pours poison into the king's ear, and leaves. The queen returns, finds her husband dead, and gives expression of grief. The murderer returns and, after the king's body has been carried away, woos the queen. At first she resists his attentions, but soon accepts his love.

In answer to Ophelia's question, Hamlet assures her that the actor who enters to speak the lines of the prologue will "tell all" – that is, explain the significance of the action. When the four lines of the prologue are recited, Ophelia remarks that it is brief. "As woman's love," Hamlet replies. The performance of the play then commences.

The action in *The Murder of Gonzago* is the same as that depicted in the dumb-show up to the point where the murderer, identified as one Lucianus, nephew to the king, pours the poison in the king's ear. The queen is emphatic in her declaration never to remarry should she become a widow. In the words of the player-king, spoken as he is about to "beguile/The tedious day with sleep," "'Tis deeply sworn."

The brief interlude gives Hamlet the opportunity to ask Gertrude how she likes the play. "The lady protests too much," she replies. Claudius then asks Hamlet if he is familiar with the dramatic story and if it is in any way an offense. The Prince replies: "No, no, they do but jest, poison in jest. No offence i' th' world." Again in reply to a question by Claudius, he explains that the play is called "The Mouse-trap." The Prince's words to Ophelia especially reveal his state of excitement. He calls upon the actor playing the role of the murderer to stop grimacing and begin to speak his lines. All along he has been, as Ophelia says, "a good chorus." When the murderer pours the poison into the player-king's ear, he assures the audience that this is the dramatization of an actual murder and that they will see how the murderer "gets the love of Gonzago's wife."

Alarmed, Claudius rises. Polonius calls for an end of the play. The King cries out: "Give me some light. Away!" All but Hamlet and Horatio leave the hall. It is a triumphant Prince who, after reciting a bit of doggerel and indulging in ironic banter with Horatio, declares that he will "take the ghost's word for a thousand pound." Horatio agrees that the King reacted like a guilty man.

Rosencrantz and Guildenstern return to inform Hamlet that the King is greatly disturbed and that the Queen wishes to speak with her son privately. In his state of high excitement, the Prince takes special pleasure in confusing the two. Aware that they tend to believe that personal ambition explains his behavior, Hamlet explains that he lacks "advancement." Especially his ironic remarks reveal his contempt for so-called friends who will not be forthright with him and presume to think that they can "pluck out the heart of [his] mystery." Polonius enters with the same message for Hamlet: the Queen wishes to speak with him. Again the Prince adopts the antic style, voicing absurd irrelevancies before he informs the Lord Chamberlain that he will honor his mother's request. He is then left to himself.

Now Hamlet's words, spoken in soliloquy, reveal a bloodthirsty mood. But he counsels himself not to inflict physical harm upon his mother, to whose chamber he will now go: "Let me be cruel, not unnatural," he says.

Commentary

Hamlet's advice to the players, which takes up some fifty lines, seems on the surface to be interesting primarily not for what it contributes to *The Tragedy of Hamlet* but for what one learns about Shakespeare, the professional actor and playwright concerned that actors do justice to his script. Scholars have pointed out that a rival company of actors was noted for splitting the ears of the groundlings, those less affluent members of the audience who stood in the pit of the theater, pandering to those who confused bombast with eloquence and realism. That there is a personal element here seems likely, especially when Hamlet says, "And let those that play your clowns speak no more than is set down for them" (42-44), counsel hardly applicable to actors performing *The Murder of Gonzago.*

This episode also provides a desirable release of tension after the disturbing nunnery scene. And again it provides evidence of Hamlet's breadth of character and normal interests. He is shown to have been a young man who enjoyed the theater and as one whose critical judgment has been highly developed. If nothing else, this tends to refute the theory that the Prince was the complete introvert unduly given to introspection, just as it adds somewhat to his intellectual stature.

Hamlet's chief concern in this episode is that *The Murder of Gonzago* be so performed that it will be a convincing imitation of life itself and, in this sense, will hold "the mirror up to nature." Only then can he be sure that it will provide the test of Claudius' conscience. If an unskillful player oversteps "the modesty of nature," presenting a "whirlwind of passion" which "out-herods Herod" (a character in the mystery plays notorious for bombast), the performance cannot possibly impress the courtly audience as worthy of serious consideration.

But there is more here. At another level, Hamlet is providing a commentary on mankind in general and making a plea for the use of God-given reason and a concern for truth as opposed to appearance. In a word, let man vindicate his supposed status as a "wondrous work" and the "paragon of animals." When the Prince speaks of holding the mirror up to nature, one inevitably recalls Ophelia's encomium of a Hamlet who had been the "glass of fashion and the mould of form" (III.i.161). Moreover, this episode looks foward to Hamlet's praise of Horatio as one who is not passion's slave.

Hamlet's praise of Horatio (59-79) has been accepted by a great many commentators as the passage which establishes Horatio as the norm character in relation to the tragic hero—that is, as the individual in the play who possesses the very qualities which Hamlet should have if he is to avoid tragic downfall. The young man whom the Prince so much admires is depicted as the true Stoic, one who accepts "Fortune's buffets" (strokes of ill fortune) with equanimity because he maintains proper balance between "blood and judgement" (74) — that is, between emotion and reason — and thus is not "passion's slave." One can understand why many believe this passage provides a key to the interpretation of *The Tragedy of Hamlet*. To be sure, the commoner Horatio, admirable as he is, has never been put to a test comparable in magnitude to that which Hamlet faces: tragic heroes must be tested and the test must be a great one.

Hamlet requests Horatio to watch the King closely to see if Claudius' "occulted [hidden] guilt/Do not itself unkennel in one speech" (85-86). It is of some interest to know that the Prince now has *his* spy. At Elsinore, where "seeming" and the use of indirections are commonplace, he will fight fire with fire, as it were. Ophelia has been "loosed" upon him; now he will have Horatio help in "unkenneling" Claudius' secret. His words reveal at least a premonition of the King's guilt; but then, since they are expressed in a conditional clause and since Hamlet goes on to consider the possibility that his "imaginations are as foul/As Vulcan's stithy" (88-89), the element of doubt relating to the nature of the Ghost is stressed once more. The question which disturbs some commentators remains: is it an assumption of the play that the establishment of Claudius' guilt proves that Hamlet saw and listened to an "honest" ghost, not to an evil spirit, perhaps the Devil himself, who used a truth to make possible Hamlet's death and damnation?

As all prepare to see the play, Hamlet's state of high excitement comes through. "I must be idle," he says to Horatio (95), and this is a cue that he will adopt the antic pose again. This pose gives him the opportunity to make remarks to the King, to Polonius, and to Ophelia which may be interpreted as evidence of mental instability and, at the same time, serve to perplex a vitally concerned listener like Claudius. It may even be argued that, at this moment shortly before the Mouse-trap is sprung, Hamlet is close to the breaking point. His reply to the King's apparently gracious concern for how Hamlet "fares" is calculated to strengthen the ambition theory first advanced by Rosencrantz and Guildenstern:

> Excellent, i' faith, — of the chameleon's dish. I eat
> the air, promise-cramm'd. You cannot feed capons
> so.
>
> (98-100)

No one should underestimate Claudius' intelligence; he is fully aware of the play upon the word *air* (heir) and of Hamlet's tacit reference to the fact that his uncle, not Hamlet himself, succeeded the late King. One satirical barb suffices for the time being. Hamlet next turns to Polonius, giving the Lord Chamberlain an opportunity to boast about his talent as an actor, indeed as one who once created the role of Julius Caesar in a university production. It will be recalled that Polonius has taken pride in skillful acting almost from the first, thus his directions first to Reynaldo and then to Ophelia, both of whom he coached on how to act their respective parts. One other point can be made in this connection. When Hamlet is told that Caesar was killed by Brutus, he replies: "It was a brute part of him to kill so capital a calf there" (110-12). For the Prince to refer to Polonius as a calf is consistent with his calling him a "fishmonger" and "that great baby . . . not yet out of his swathing-clouts"; that is, it is another expression of contempt for this foolish old counselor. But not long hereafter, Polonius, engaged in another spying expedition, will be slain; and it will be Hamlet himself who will play the brute part. Shakespeare provides a bit of dramatic presaging here.

For his purpose, Hamlet must find a place where he can closely watch Claudius. But in his reply to Gertrude's invitation that he sit next to her, he is able to contribute to Polonius' theory; that is, he is mad for the love of Ophelia. The bawdy remarks he makes to that young lady carry forward the theme of honesty in women. "You are merry, my lord," says Ophelia. Hamlet's reply reveals his state of tension and his disillusionment. "O God, your only jig-maker" (132) may be paraphrased as "life is a farce." His lines which follow are packed with bitterness, and his ironic reference to the length of man's memory may be an indictment not only of Gertrude but also of himself: "remember me," the Ghost had intoned repeatedly. Hamlet, who had then declared that he would sweep to his revenge without delay, is reminded in this episode that four months have elapsed since his father's death.

Especially in pre-Shakespearean drama, the dumb-show was used to indicate action which was not presented in the play proper or to symbolize what was to be presented. The dumb-show here poses certain problems. It is certainly not one of those "inexplicable dumb-shows" Hamlet had criticized earlier (13). It includes most of the circumstances of the murder as told by the Ghost, although it includes nothing suggesting that Gertrude was unfaithful to King Hamlet when he was alive or that she was involved in the murder. Why did Shakespeare include this dumb-show? Why is not Claudius startled and aroused by it? These have been abiding questions among Shakespearean critics.

Since the play-within-a-play is written advisedly in an artificial style in contrast to the play proper, Shakespeare may have added the dumb-show to intensify the contrasting elements– so a few critics have believed. But, although Ophelia suggests that it may impart the argument (150), such was not the practice among English dramatists. Then why should Shakespeare depart radically from the usual practice if he wished only to provide contrast? This has led to other conjectures. One is that Hamlet, who has arranged for the entire production, includes the dumb-show so that he will have a double opportunity of catching the conscience of the King. Another is that Hamlet did not anticipate the dumb-show and is annoyed at its presentation. A third is that Claudius pays no attention to the preliminary stage business, occupying himself, perhaps, in low-voiced talk with Gertrude. Thus he asks a bit later, "Have you heard the argument? Is there no offence in't?" (242-43). And, since all this is in the realm of conjecture, one may argue that Claudius, no ordinary villain, exercised supreme control during the dumb-show, a control he could not sustain when, in the play itself, Lucianus pours poison into the ear of the sleeping player-king. Whatever the answer may be, one thing is indisputable. Shakespeare achieves a dramatic master stroke, a moment of supreme excitement, when the King rises in fright and cries out: "Give me some light. Away!" (280). The Mouse-trap has been sprung; Hamlet has caught the conscience of the King.

The Prince's reaction is not one of horror but of elation — understandably because, despite his expression of doubt, he now has absolute proof of Claudius' guilt. Perhaps he is relieved especially because he can act as one executing public justice, not just as a son carrying out blood revenge in accordance with an old, barbaric code. The difficulty, however, is that nowhere in the play does Hamlet explicitly question the propriety of revenge. One is reminded that some critics believe that Shakespeare was unable to surmount the basic difficulties of transmuting the earlier Hamlet material when he provided an unmistakably Christian framework for his dramatic version. The Ghost spoke truly: Claudius is guilty of fratricide and regicide. But is Hamlet to emerge as minister (one righteously carrying out God's vengeance upon a heinous sinner) or as scourge (one whose sinful act of taking vengeance into his own hands God permits for His own purpose, but who ultimately will face God's punishment). Again, it should be noted, Hamlet's prime concern has been to establish Claudius' guilt, not the "honesty" of the Ghost. All this deserves notice if one is to do justice to *The Tragedy of Hamlet* and to understand why it has been subject to apparently endless discussion. But this is not to deny that readers and audiences have not the slightest doubt that Hamlet, Prince of Denmark, should slay Claudius and remove the source of all rottenness in the State.

Exactly which lines Hamlet composed for insertion into *The Murder of Gonzago* is not known. But there are lines spoken by the player-king which seem to have direct applicability to Hamlet and his problem, certainly not to Claudius. Consider lines 197-207, beginning "But what we do determine oft we break." Hamlet's announced purpose to move swiftly to revenge his father's murder was of "violent birth" and, especially in his second soliloquy (II.ii.576 ff.), he had questioned, in effect, whether or not his purpose lacked "validity" (strength) since Claudius survived and even seemed to flourish. The player-king's words on passion (204-7) may be a kind of indictment of Hamlet; some who see the Prince as the slave of extreme melancholy particularly think so.

Hamlet's mood of excitement and elation is sustained in the first part of his dialogue with Rosencrantz and Guildenstern, one of whom informs him that the King is "In his retirement marvellous distemper'd" (312). "With drink, sir?" asks Hamlet, and one is reminded of his "dram of evil" speech, voiced when he waited for the appearance of the Ghost (I.iv.13 ff.). In this current display of the antic disposition, his discourse, wild though it sounds to the King's spies, shows method and basic rationality. Especially this comes through when, after stating that he will obey his mother's request, he asks, "Have you any further trade with us?" — advisedly using the plural form of the pronoun and thus presenting himself to them not as a former schoolfellow and as a friend, but as the Prince of Denmark (347). His use of irony is quite bitter and penetrating when he assures Rosencrantz and Guildenstern "by these pickers and stealers" that he still loves them. In an earlier scene, when they first sought him out, Hamlet had spoken of handshaking as the "appurtenance of welcome" employed as a matter of fashion and ceremony (II.ii.388-89); his reference here to hands and fingers as "pickers and stealers" is far more devastating. Apparently Hamlet enjoys misleading these two. "Sir, I lack advancement," he says to Rosencrantz; and then he concludes with a reference to a proverb that is indeed musty: "While the grass grows . . . " (358). But it is quite possible that the Prince is again being ironical; he may well be expressing a strong desire to get on with the act of revenge.

When one of the players reenters with a recorder (an old type of flute), Hamlet, deadly serious, finds an even more devastating way of showing his contempt for Guildenstern. His longer speech at this point has wider application. Guildenstern states that he lacks the skill to play a recorder; yet he is presumptuous enough to think that he can "play" upon Hamlet, as the latter makes abundantly clear:

> 'Sblood,
> do you think that I am easier to be play'd on than a
> pipe? Call me what instrument you will, though
> you can fret me, you cannot play upon me.
>
> (385-88)

In his praise of his true friend Horatio, Hamlet had lauded those who "are not a pipe for Fortune's finger/To sound what stop she please" (75-76). Now, having forced Claudius to reveal his guilt, perhaps Hamlet is announcing his right to be numbered as one of those. But surely, in terms of the entire play, there is more here. The late Aldous Huxley wrote provocatively that Hamlet, an idealist dedicated to truth, alone knew that man could be a whole orchestra, not just a simple pipe to be played on. If that reading is correct, then Hamlet, with his gift for universalizing, speaks for man who, were he to realize his potential, indeed is the paragon of animals, like unto the angels. Only the pragmatic, earth-bound and self-seeking, be they high-placed or not, reject their heritage and imitate humanity so abominably in the theater of life.

Polonius, that easy target for Hamlet's barbs, enters. Once more he is the bearer of stale news, and once more this old counselor renders himself ridiculous. He does, however, get an answer from the Prince; Hamlet will come to his mother by and by. And then, just before all but Hamlet leave, the latter says, somewhat ambiguously, " 'By and by' is easily said" (404). It is possible that he is showing again his awareness of having found occasion to delay.

So far in this scene, Hamlet has manifested first the mood of the decisive, composed intellectual in his advice to the players; next, the mood of the generous-minded and idealistic friend in his warm praise of Horatio; then the mood of satirical gaiety in his words to the King, Polonius, and Ophelia; and last, the mood of contempt and aloofness in his words to Rosencrantz and Guildenstern. Now, speaking in soliloquy at the end of this climactic scene, he provides a prime example of a shocking shift in emotion. This is not the Hamlet who exclaimed "O cursed spite,/That ever I was born to set it right!"—the Hamlet who recoiled at the thought of being called upon to execute vengeance. Rather it is the Hamlet who, immediately after hearing the Ghost's story, inveighed against Gertrude ("O most pernicious woman!") and Claudius ("O villain, villain, smiling, damned villain!"). It is the Hamlet who, in his second soliloquy, after having denounced himself as "a rogue and peasant slave," cried out:

> Bloody, bawdy villain!
> Remorseless, treacherous, lecherous, kindless villain!
> O, vengeance!
>
> (II.ii 608-10)

If anything, his words here are even more greatly overwrought, what with the reference to yawning churchyards (open graves), hell's contagion, and (the very language of a Black Mass) drinking hot blood. These are words one would expect to hear not from the gifted hero of a high tragedy but rather from the protagonist in a melodramatic revenge play; they are not those of a tragic hero intent upon executing public justice, but of an individual determined to carry out blood revenge come what may. Yet Shakespeare has provided motivation, and Hamlet's emotional stress is understandable. At the same time, it would seem that the dramatist exhibits in this passage a hero who is far from being able to accept "Fortune's buffets and rewards . . . with equal thanks"; in terms of the high standard of personal control which he found exemplified in Horatio, Hamlet is enslaved by passion.

But, characteristically, Hamlet checks himself: "Soft! now to my mother./O heart, lose not thy nature" (410-11). Nor does one find here another excuse for delay, for Rosencrantz and Guildenstern had reported that the King was inaccessible. That his mother's sin remains a great part of his tragedy is re-emphasized. Hamlet prays that he will not follow the example of the matricidal Nero. He will "be cruel, not unnatural"; he will "speak daggers to her, but use none" (411-14).

ACT III – SCENE 3

Summary

The King informs Rosencrantz and Guildenstern that, since it is unsafe to let Hamlet's "madness range," they are commissioned to conduct the Prince to England as soon as possible. Guildenstern and Rosencrantz express their dedication to the service of the King and their conviction that the welfare of the State depends upon his health and safety. They assure the King that they will waste no time in carrying out his instructions.

Polonius enters and reports that Hamlet is going to his mother's chamber and that he himself will hide behind the arras (wall hanging of tapestry) to hear what is said. Claudius thanks him, and the Lord Chamberlain departs.

Alone, a conscience-stricken Claudius reveals his thoughts. He identifies himself with Cain, the first murderer and the first fratricide, and asks himself whether or not, in view of the magnitude of his crime, he can hope for divine mercy. He answers his own question: Christian mercy is denied to no one who is truly penitent. But he knows full well that penance is more than the expression of regret; restitution, to the extent possible, is necessary. Since he will not give up either the crown or his dead brother's wife, the efficacy of prayer is denied him. In despair and torment he cries out: "Help, angels! Make assay!" (69). And he expresses the fervent hope that "All may be well" (72) as he kneels in an attempt to pray.

Hamlet enters with drawn sword but restrains himself from slaying Claudius because his father was killed before he could be shriven of his sins, venial and/or mortal. Hamlet is determined that Claudius die in a state of sin: hell, not heaven or even purgatory, must be his destination. The Prince leaves for his mother's chamber. The King rises, aware that his words "fly up" but that his "thoughts remain below."

Commentary

Claudius' soliloquy provides a second and far more detailed self-acknowledgment of guilt. As was said with reference to the first soliloquy (III.i.50-54), villain though he is, Claudius (like Macbeth and in contrast to such a dedicated sinner as Richard III) possesses a conscience, one which hardly makes him cowardly but rather makes him an erring human being, not an inhuman monster. Claudius clearly is not a born villain; nor, however much he has sought to conceal his real self from others, does he seek to avoid moral and religious truth. He is orthodox and well schooled in Christian doctrine, fully aware that, so long as he holds on to what he has gained through acts of mortal sin, he cannot purge his soul of guilt. In his anguish he is indeed a "limed soul." At this particular moment in the action, it is possible to feel some pity for this tormented man despite his appalling crimes.

The Hamlet whose thoughts are revealed when he comes upon Claudius kneeling in an attempt to pray has startled and offended one commentator after another over the years, so vindictive does he seem to be. In an attempt to explain Hamlet's words which, some insist, make any humane person recoil, that ever-present means for resolving doubts has been used again: tradition—the original Hamlet story and the pattern established by typical Elizabethan and Jacobean revenge plays— asserts itself. It is undeniable that personal hatred, not just the concern for executing justice, motivates the Prince in this speech. He would see his adversary eternally damned, not just deprived of mortality. But if it is possible to find sympathy for Claudius the tormented sinner, it is possible to understand Hamlet's inability to shake off the personal wrath against the man who killed his father and whored his mother.

Among the Romantics, all this is held to be another and, in this instance, crucial example of Hamlet's vacillation. It is argued that, so far from Hamlet's expressing a terrible resolve to kill Claudius in a state of sin, he is indulging in self-deception, grasping at another excuse for delay. Romantics (and other critics, for that matter) long since have found here the turning-point in the play. Indeed, had Hamlet slain Claudius in this scene, all other violent deaths, especially that of the tragic hero, would not have occurred. In reply, one may point out the obvious: the play would end prematurely and it would not be *The Tragedy of Hamlet* but rather a very unsatisfactory melodrama which ends abruptly after tantalizing the audience by introducing profound questions and complexities of character. More telling is this question: who would like to have a Hamlet who, in a bloodthirsty mood, swept to his revenge, slaughtering the kneeling King? Despite all that one has learned about him up to this point in the action, Hamlet could not win sympathy; such a bloody act would lead to the conclusion that indeed a noble mind had been overthrown.

A last point may be made. Ironically, Hamlet is restrained by the belief that Claudius is making a "good" confession and thus escaping damnation. Thanks to the convention of the soliloquy, one is aware that he is unable to do so.

ACT III – SCENE 4

Summary

Polonius, good as his word, has preceded Hamlet to the Queen's chamber and now instructs her to be firm with her son. He hides behind the arras just before the Prince enters.

Gertrude begins firmly to reprove her son, but his replies and his insistence that she sit down and listen to him so frighten her that she calls out for help. From behind the arras, Polonius echoes her cry. Promptly Hamlet draws his rapier, runs it through the arras, and kills the Lord Chamberlain. "Is it the King?" he asks his distraught mother. But Gertrude can only exclaim upon the monstrosity of the deed. Fiercely Hamlet replies: "Almost as bad, good mother,/As kill a king, and marry with his brother" (28-29). Only then does he lift up the arras and reveal the dead Polonius, whom he describes as a fool.

The Prince then begins to castigate Gertrude. He shows her contrasting portraits, one of King Hamlet, whom he lauds, the other of Claudius, whom he execrates. How, he asks, could she have given herself to Claudius? Hamlet, in effect, answers his own question, accusing his mother of lustfulness. The tormented Gertrude implores him to speak no more.

Suddenly the Ghost appears – but only to Hamlet, who is sure that it comes to reprove him for his delay. Solemnly the Ghost says that it comes "to whet [Hamlet's] almost blunted purpose" (111). But immediately it expresses concern for Gertrude, who is convinced that her son has lost his mind. At its behest, Hamlet speaks gently to his mother, but becomes highly excited in his effort to convince her of the presence of King Hamlet's spirit. The Ghost departs.

When Gertrude expresses her conviction that her son is the victim of a hallucination, Hamlet replies that it is not madness that he has spoken and implores her to acknowledge her guilt, confessing herself to heaven. At least, he says, let her assume a virtue, or take the first step toward virtue by avoiding further cohabitation with Claudius. Now in a calmer mood, the Prince points to the body of Polonius and voices his regret for the death of the Lord Chamberlain. He bids his mother good-night and adds that he must be cruel only to be kind. But when she asks what she must do, his reply is bitterly ironic: let her return in wantonness to Claudius; let her report that he is "mad in craft." Is that not the duty of a loving queen? Gertrude vows that she will not breathe a word of what her son has said to her.

Hamlet tells his mother that he is being sent to England, accompanied by his two schoolfellows whom he completely distrusts. Convinced that they function as agents for his destruction, he will turn the tables on them. In this mood of violent determination, the Prince callously states that he will remove Polonius' body: "I'll lug the guts into the neighbour room." Again he bids Gertrude goodnight.

Commentary

It is upon this scene in particular that the neo-Freudians depend for support of their explanation of Hamlet's conduct, since here the tragic hero does manifest an overwhelming concern about Gertrude's sexual life. They find in this scene a Hamlet moved not by idealism and the Renaissance concept of family honor but by consuming jealousy due to his unconscious, incestuous love for his mother. For them, Hamlet's hatred of Claudius results from the fact that Claudius — rather than Hamlet himself — killed the King. In contrast to the neo-Freudians, the orthodox Shakespeareans, who never forget that Shakespeare was a man of the Renaissance, find in this scene a Hamlet who is a moral idealist and who neither exaggerates Gertrude's guilt nor indulges in self-righteousness.

It is quite possible that the neo-Freudian interpretation of *Hamlet* was popularized by the Lawrence Olivier motion picture version of the play, which dates from the late forties. There, Gertrude and her son were depicted sitting upon a bed, the satin coverlet of which was arranged in voluptuous folds, when the two engaged in emotionally charged discourse. A closet, be it that of the Queen or of Ophelia (mentioned earlier in the play), was a private sitting room, sometimes a sewing room but never a bedroom. In this scene it is the private chamber to which Gertrude, with lady attendants on occasion, could retire.

In his counsel to Gertrude, Polonius urges her to let Hamlet know that "his pranks have been too broad to bear with" (2). It is probable that he refers specifically to the Prince's remarks about a second marriage made in the course of the Mouse-trap play. When the Lord

Chamberlain goes on to say "I'll silence me e'en here" (4), Shakespeare achieves dramatic irony, probably well appreciated by his audience since the basic story elements were almost as well known as those of *Romeo and Juliet.*

Up to this scene, the extent of Gertrude's guilt has not been made clear. Now it may be concluded that she knew nothing about the murder of King Hamlet. She is appalled when Hamlet draws his rapier and drives the blade through the arras, killing Polonius. But her horror and surprise are just as great when Hamlet picks up her words and goes on to excoriate her:

> A bloody deed! Almost as bad, good mother,
> As kill a king, and marry his brother.
>
> (28-29)

To paraphrase the Ghost's words when it first spoke to Hamlet, Gertrude is the weak vessel, deficient in moral insight and therefore susceptible to the importunings of Claudius. This estimate of her character finds support especially when her son, directing her to look upon the portraits of King Hamlet and Claudius, asks: "Ha! have you eyes?" (67). Only with reluctance can she move just a step toward moral awareness and self-criticism:

> O, speak to me no more
> These words like daggers enter in mine ears.
> No more, sweet Hamlet!
>
> (94-96)

Although she assures the Prince that she will not breathe a word of what has been said (197-99), she does not promise to avoid further intimacy with Claudius. When the Ghost appears to Hamlet, Gertrude exclaims: "Alas, he's mad!" (105). Under the circumstances, her reaction is a natural one; but may not this serve to relieve her of the tormenting belief that Hamlet spoke truly to her, however cruelly? Her conduct in subsequent scenes tends to support such a conclusion.

The range of emotions which Hamlet exhibits in this scene is great indeed. After concluding the "shenting" of Gertrude with a caustic indictment of "the bloat king," he practically gloats over the prospect of outdoing in craft Rosencrantz and Guildenstern, the willing servants of Claudius. He will thrust them as he would "adders fang'd"; they will "marshal [him] to knavery":

> For 'tis the sport to have the engineer
> Hoist with his own petar;
>
> (206-7)

Here speaks a Hamlet who is far from being "A man that Fortune's buffets and rewards" takes "with equal thanks," but rather one who is prepared to "drink hot blood." However aware one is that Hamlet has "great cause," one should not ignore the fact that he is far from the ideal of which he declared Horatio to be the exemplar (III.ii.68 ff.).

Many of the Prince's lines seem to be as cruel as those he addressed to Ophelia in the nunnery scene, although the motivation is sounder since he has sprung the Mouse-trap and is addressing a mother notoriously lax in conduct. From the start, his tone is harsh enough to make Gertrude fear for her life. (There is no textual evidence that he threatens her with physical violence; the traditional stage directions indicate that he draws his sword only when he hears Polonius cry out from behind the arras.) "How now! A rat?" he asks—and one is forcibly reminded of the Mouse-trap set for Claudius. Once discovering that he has killed the elderly Lord Chamberlain, his remarks are callous and perfunctory:

> Thou wretched, rash, intruding fool, farewell!
> I took thee for thy better. Take thy fortune.
> Thou find'st to be too busy is some danger.
>
> (31-33)

Turning to Gertrude, Hamlet says coldly: "Leave wringing of your hands."

At the end of the scene, Hamlet's mood is determined not only by thoughts of the marriage bed but also by the "knavery" of Rosencrantz and Guildenstern. He speaks even more unfeelingly: "I'll lug the guts into the neighbour room" (212). Then he indulges himself in irony at the expense of the once-voluble Polonius, that "foolish prating knave." To be sure, one is aware that, in a sense, Polonius silenced himself— that is, he was an engineer hoisted by "his own petar," paying a steep price for his underhanded methods and overconfidence. But to assume that Hamlet has executed public justice simply will not do, as the Prince's own words, to be noted below, make clear.

Little wonder that *Hamlet* has been called the most problematic play ever written and that the tragic hero's world has been described as one that is predominantly interrogative in mood. The discussion above does not exhaust the questions posed in this scene. In the preceding scene, Hamlet had been restrained from killing his uncle-king only by vindictiveness, a determination not only to take the life of his adversary but also to insure Claudius' damnation. Now, acting impulsively, he strikes with his sword, convinced that its blade will reach the King. How could he explain the violent death? Would the testimony of the commoner Horatio be sufficient to clear his treasured reputation for honor? More important, would a subdued, rational Hamlet be satisfied that his motive for revenge was not tainted by a personal hatred outweighing public duty? These are questions which have been raised and which should not be ignored. So intense is Hamlet's detestation of Claudius that, in this scene, his invectives match those he used in the first and second soliloquies; but here they are amplified. Claudius is not only "A king of shreds and patches" (102); he is the "bloat king," a "paddock [toad]," a "bat," and a "gib [tom-cat]." The bestial images are used to represent extreme, loathsome sensuality.

All this is developed most effectively when Hamlet calls upon Gertrude to look at the pictures, the "counterfeit presentment of two brothers" (53-65). His words relate back to two important, earlier passages in the play, his first soliloquy and his advice to the players. In the soliloquy, the Prince provided the initial contrast between his father and Claudius, deploring the sensuality of his mother which led to the incestuous marriage:

> So excellent a king; that was, to this,
> Hyperion to a satyr . . .
> . . . .
> My father's brother, but no more like my father
> Than I to Hercules; . . .
>
> (I.ii.139-40/52-53)

In his advice to the players, Hamlet urged them not to overstep "the modesty of nature" but rather to hold "the mirror up to nature," showing "virtue her own feature, scorn her own image" (III.ii.18 ff.). To Hamlet, Claudius, whose portrait contrasts so unfavorably with that of the dead ruler, imitates humanity abominably. Now King Hamlet is identified with four gods of the classical Pantheon:

> See, what a grace was seated on his brow:
> Hyperion's curls, the front of Jove himself,
> An eye like Mars, to threaten or command,
> A station like the herald Mercury
> New-lighted on a heaven-kissing hill. . . .
>
> (55-59)

"This was your husband," he continues; and then he directs her attention to the picture of Claudius: "Here is your husband, like a mildew'd ear,/Blasting his wholesome brother." When the Prince goes on to compare Claudius to a "moor" upon which Gertrude now "battens" (gorges herself), he is strongly emphasizing appetite as opposed to reason.

Hamlet had ended his first soliloquy with a lament: "But break my heart, for I must hold my tongue" (I.ii.159). The antic disposition did give him opportunities to express his heartfelt thoughts covertly, but never directly, to his mother and only rarely to his uncle-king. Having sprung the Mouse-trap and proved to his own satisfaction that Claudius, once an object of derision (II.ii.380-83) but now the powerful ruler of Denmark, is guilty of regicide and usurpation, he need not suffer in silence. Claudius now is fully aware that Hamlet has ferreted out his secret; in the dramatization of *The Murder of Gonzago* he saw a portrait of himself. It is now Gertrude's turn to see her true image. That Hamlet believed Claudius (whose inaccessibility had been reported to him) was hiding in Gertrude's chamber just might be the immediate reason for his outburst; so a few have reasoned. But even if that were true, it does not follow that the Prince is motivated by an overpowering Oedipal urge to slay Claudius.

All this, however, is not to deny that Hamlet dwells upon the theme of lechery with an emphasis, and in such detail, that some find him to be fascinated by the very thing which nauseates him. The hasty marriage of Claudius and Gertrude was an incestuous one according to the Christian doctrine which informs this play, a fact which is worth repeating. Hamlet is the son of a father whom he revered not only as godlike — but as a *man,* with all the far-reaching implications of that monosyllabic term (see I.ii.188-89). Above all, Gertrude's frailty is a stain upon the cherished honor of the royal family. But for Hamlet, with his propensity for universalizing, it transcends the family level, staining all mankind. "Man delights not me," the Prince had said to Rosencrantz and Guildenstern, — "no, nor woman neither, though by your smiling you seem to say so" (II.ii.321-22). Related to all this is the established fact that, in the mature Shakespeare (as elsewhere in much of the serious literature of the period), illicit sex was a symbol of pervading evil. Hamlet's apparent obsession with the sensual, amounting to what has been called sexual nausea, is no more an indication of abnormality than is King Lear's ironic defense of adultery. Consider the Prince's reply to Gertrude when she asks why he berates her:

> Such an act
> That blurs the grace and blush of modesty,
> Calls virtue hypocrite, takes off the rose
> From the fair forehead of an innocent love
> And sets a blister there, makes marriage vows
> As false as dicers' oaths.
>
> (40-45)

"Sets a blister," as here used, means "brands as a harlot." One immediately recalls the nunnery scene. For the Lord Chamberlain's daughter had been "loosed" upon Hamlet, and to him she was not "honest"; in a sense, she was being prostituted by an unprincipled father in the service of the satyr-like Claudius. Yet he surely knew that Ophelia was a hapless victim. The source of the corruption was the King, who had won over Gertrude as a partner in an unholy union. And that was an act which the idealistic Christian Prince finds to be so monstrous that it admits to generalization with reference to mankind and especially to man's brave claim to being the paragon of animals.

Hamlet indeed has spoken daggers in his "shenting" of Gertrude. But when the Ghost appears and not only rebukes him for procrastination but also urges him to "step between [Gertrude] and her fighting soul" (113), Hamlet seems to be aware that he has violated the Ghost's earlier admonition—tainting his mind by striving against his mother, instead of leaving her to heaven. Not without compassion, he now implores her not to interpret his words as evidence of madness and thus an excuse for her to ignore her guilt. Rather, let her confess herself to heaven, or at the very least avoid compounding her sin by going to Claudius' bed (144-70).

In this calmer mood, the Prince now can express repentance for the slaying of Polonius and declare that he will not shirk from reporting the deed honestly. Yet his words are of special interest:

> but Heaven hath pleas'd it so,
> To punish me with this and this with me,
> That I must be their scourge and minister.
> (173-75)

A scourge, it will be recalled, is a wicked person who adds to his evil deeds even while functioning as the instrument of God's vengeance; ultimately he will fall and will endure eternal damnation. A minister is the virtuous instrument of God's justice. Is it possible for anyone to be both scourge and minister? Among many theories advanced by Shakespearean critics, this question is as important as any other one. It is quite possible that the poet-dramatist intends to show that the tragic hero himself is still in doubt regarding the morality of the task which remains to be performed. One recalls Hamlet's words of despair uttered at the end of Act I, where he first encountered the Ghost, listened to its story, and received the injunction to avenge the death of King Hamlet:

> The time is out of joint;—O cursed spite,
> That ever I was born to set it right!
> (I.v.189-90)

It may be argued that Hamlet's words in both the earlier and the present scene serve to illuminate the dilemma he has faced practically from the start: is it possible to accept as a moral duty the execution of revenge upon Claudius without tainting his own mind? Should he be the Pyrrhus-type revenger, the man of blood and passion, prompt in action, undeterred by the processes of thought? In a moment of passion he acted without the slightest delay, with the result that the underhanded, foolish, but certainly not archcriminal Polonius was killed—the act of a scourge, not of a noble mind called upon to function as God's minister. His passion inflamed again when he makes his reply to Gertrude's question "What shall I do?" (180), Hamlet then expresses his determination to outdo Rosencrantz and Guildenstern in knavery. So great are the difficulties of conduct in his world where Claudius is King and Polonius was accepted as the wisest counselor, a world of vice and hypocrisy, that the Prince cannot avoid being the pawn of Fortune. This, at least, is the protagonist who, for many students of the play, emerges at the end of Act III.

Finally, the Ghost in this scene demands attention, especially because this time only Hamlet sees it. First, why does it make its last appearance at this particular place and only to one of the two persons present? A widely accepted theory is that it does so because Hamlet is doing something that he should not do — speaking daggers to the woman who should be left to heaven. Such an action, so the argument goes, would be proper for the spirit of the Hyperion-like King Hamlet; moreover, it would be the action of a benevolent spirit, an "honest" ghost. But it also has been argued that, since Gertrude does not see or hear the Ghost and therefore believes her son to be mad, the Ghost's appearance only to Hamlet serves to defeat her intention to repent. If this reading is valid, then the Ghost may be malignant. When the Prince first sees it, he exclaims: "Save me, and hover o'er me with your wings,/You heavenly guards!" (103-4). This is a variation of the orthodox Christian formula to be used when one sees a ghost; it is similar to what Hamlet voiced on the platform at Elsinore (I.iv.39). One may reasonably ask why he should use this formula if he really is convinced that this is "a spirit of health," not a "goblin damn'd." Still another conjecture is that Gertrude cannot see the Ghost because she is a grievous sinner.

An indisputable reason for the Ghost's appearance, acknowledged by Hamlet and confirmed by the Ghost itself, is to reprove the Prince for delaying the revenge. Just possibly its appearance may be due to Hamlet's failure to take advantage of the opportunity when Claudius knelt in an attempt to pray. However, one may well ask: would a benevolent spirit have approved of action under such circumstances?

Other commentators point out another disturbing possibility. May not Hamlet, in a state of great passion, actually be experiencing a hallucination, the reflection of his own state of mind? Although this theory is not generally accepted, it cannot be dismissed summarily as just another flight into the stratosphere of impressionistic criticism. The startled Prince addresses the Ghost in these words:

> Do you not come your tardy son to chide,
> That, laps'd in time and passion, lets go by
> Th' important acting of your dread command?
>
> (106-8)

These words of self-accusation, so it has been argued, are motivated by Hamlet's failure to kill Claudius when he had his chance shortly after springing the Mouse-trap. Further, Hamlet repeats in essence just what he said about himself earlier, notably when he denounced himself as being "A dull and muddy-mettled rascal . . . unpregnant of [his] cause" (II.ii.594-95) and referred to his "weakness" and his "melancholy" (II.ii.630), and also in his third soliloquy when he spoke of the "native hue of resolution" being "sicklied o'er with the pale cast of thought" (III.i.84-85). Consistent with this argument is the Ghost's reply: "Do not forget! This visitation/Is but to whet thy almost blunted purpose" (110-11).

There remains only to repeat that the usual interpretation is that this is the Ghost of Hamlet's father, that Hamlet is right in believing that it has come to spur him to positive action, that its concern for Gertrude is no more than consistent with its original admonition that she should be left to heaven, and that one death—that of Claudius—will satisfy it.

ACT IV – SCENE 1

Summary

Claudius expresses concern for the emotionally disturbed Gertrude and asks where her son is. First dismissing Rosencrantz and Guildenstern, the Queen replies that Hamlet, "Mad as the seas and winds, when both contend/Which is the mightier," has killed Polonius, the "unseen good old man." The King deplores the violent deed, aware that he would have been the victim had he been behind the arras. Charging himself with being derelict for not restraining Hamlet earlier, he wonders how he will be able to explain Polonius' death to his subjects. Gertrude informs him that the Prince, lamenting his action, is removing the body of the Lord Chamberlain.

The King states that Hamlet must be sent away at once, and he calls for Guildenstern. When the latter enters with Rosencrantz, the two are told what has happened and instructed to seek out Hamlet, talk with him as if nothing had occurred, and bring Polonius' body to the chapel. They depart. Claudius then informs Gertrude that they must turn to their wisest friends and tell them what they "mean to do/And what's untimely done" (39-40). Perhaps then they will not be held accountable for the death of Polonius.

Commentary

Gertrude's explanation of what happened has been subject to contrasting interpretations. To most readers, it seems evident that she honestly believes her son to be mad because she speaks of his grief as evidence of his basic purity (24-27) and because Claudius' lines point to his awareness of her genuine love and concern for her son. Others see Gertrude as making good her promise not to reveal Hamlet's secret, but as having accepted eagerly the belief that he is mentally unbalanced as a "flattering unction to [her] soul," to use the Prince's own words (III.iv.145). By this latter group, much is made of the fact that her regard for Claudius seems to be undisturbed by Hamlet's accusations and invectives.

Claudius' words and actions in this scene pose no such problem of interpretation. In the course of the action so far in this play, his concern for his own security has been linked to Hamlet. The behavior of Hamlet now has become an obsession with him. "Ah, my good lord, what I have seen tonight!" exclaims Gertrude, and Claudius promptly asks, "How does Hamlet?" And, at the end of the scene, he says, "My soul is full of discord and dismay." But, appropriately, fear does not incapacitate Claudius; with Machiavellian skill, he expresses his conviction that Hamlet is now a threat not only to the Crown, but also to all subjects; and he blames himself for permitting his "love" for the Prince to interfere with duty. The intensity of the conflict is perhaps best indicated by the King's use of a military figure of speech when he tells Gertrude how they must report the death of Polonius.

Finally, it now seems possible that Hamlet's slaying of Polonius has worked to the advantage of his adversary. Only select members of the Court witnessed Hamlet's antic behavior and heard his antic discourse. The Prince, who, as Ophelia's encomium made clear, was the "expectancy and rose of the fair state" (III.i.160), can now be removed from Denmark without causing subjects to ask troublesome questions.

ACT IV – SCENE 2

Summary

Hamlet, adopting the same ironic and riddling style of discourse which he used earlier, refuses to tell Rosencrantz and Guildenstern where he placed the body of Polonius, but he agrees to go with them to see the King.

Commentary

Why Hamlet chooses to provoke the King and his spies by hiding Polonius' body is a bit of a puzzle. Many find here a perverseness unworthy of a tragic hero; others find further evidence of the Prince's

morbid preoccupation with death, first manifested in his soliloquy at
the end of Act I, Scene ii, and developed in the "To be, or not to be"
soliloquy in Act III, Scene i.

The Prince's utter contempt for Rosencrantz and Guildenstern finds
expression once more. Speaking to the former, he has a devastating term
to explain Rosencrantz' motive for abjectly serving Claudius: this
former schoolfellow is a sponge that "soaks up the King's countenance
[reference to the coin of the realm], his rewards, his authorities" (16-17);
like other servile individuals, the King keeps him "as an ape doth nuts,
in the corner of his jaw; first mouth'd, to be last swallowed" (19-20).
Having listened to the sanctimonious platitudes about the sanctity of
kingship (II.ii.26-29), one is hardly surprised that Guildenstern should
express shock when he hears Hamlet refer to the King as a "thing" (31).

ACT IV – SCENE 3

Summary

Addressing a small group of courtiers, Claudius states that he has
sent for Hamlet, who must not be confined, despite his dangerous
lunacy, because the "distracted multitude," lacking true judgment, love
him. The decision to exile Hamlet must be represented as the verdict
of the wisest counselors. Rosencrantz enters and reports that Hamlet
will not reveal what he has done with Polonius' body. In response to
the King's command, he calls to Guildenstern to bring in the Prince.

Questioned by the King, Hamlet replies with witty, yet cynical,
evasion. Finally, he states that Polonius' body may be found if one goes
"up the stairs into the lobby" (37-39). When told that he must be sent to
England, Hamlet continues to bait the King, bidding him "Farewell,
dear mother," and then, perhaps unnecessarily, explaining the propriety
of such a designation.

After Hamlet has left, Claudius orders Rosencrantz and Guildenstern to see to it that the Prince is aboard ship by nightfall. Left to himself, he then voices his thoughts, which are addressed to the English
ruler: Hamlet is to be put to death as soon as he arrives in England; only
then can Claudius find repose.

Commentary

Hamlet seems to take great satisfaction in capitalizing upon his pre-
tended madness; but, if anything, his wit is grimmer than ever. Again
he seems to be completely morbid in his preoccupation with death.
Questioned about Polonius' body, he develops the "worm's meat"

theme, inherited by the Renaissance from the Middle Ages, with telling effect upon Claudius. However high-spirited Hamlet may seem, however callous in his attitude toward the dead Polonius, this is the same Hamlet who, after his moving eulogy of mankind as "the beauty of the world," asked, "And yet, to me, what is this quintessence of dust?"— and then went on to declare that man did not please him (II.ii.315 ff.). It is the same Hamlet who was at least half in love with death when he gave voice to his thoughts in the "To be, or not to be" soliloquy (III.i.56 ff.). In a word, it is Hamlet the disillusioned idealist who has discovered how bestial man may become. So now he gets a perverse pleasure out of telling Claudius that

> A certain convocation of politic [politically-minded] worms are e'en at him [Polonius]. Your worm is your only emperor for diet. We fat all creatures else to fat us, and we fat ourselves for maggots. Your fat king and your lean beggar is but variable service, two dishes, but to one table; that's the end.
>
> (21-26)

In the development of the "worm's meat" theme during the Middle Ages, the aim was to inculcate the religious lesson that heaven should be recognized as man's destination and ultimate home, and that he should not be misled by whatever temporal life has to offer. But there is no consolation of religion implicit in Hamlet's grim remarks; the whole emphasis is upon man's insignificance. However nihilistic all this may seem, the Prince remains the accomplished moral satirist. For example, he achieves a metaphysical conceit and a political pun when he informs the King that:

> A man may fish with the worm that hath eat of a king, and eat of the fish that hath fed of that worm.
>
> (28-30)

and goes on to explain that all this means "Nothing but to show you how a king may go a progress through the guts of a beggar (32-33)." It would be desirable to keep this episode in mind when one comes to the graveyard scene in the last act.

Finally, Hamlet caustically bids farewell to the King, calling him his mother and going on to explain, "Father and mother is man and wife, man and wife is one flesh [as they are called in Scriptures], and so, my mother" (53-55). One is reminded that the cause of Hamlet's tragedy is two-fold. Never does he forget his father's death; but the incestuous marriage continues to torment him.

ACT IV – SCENE 4

Summary

Fortinbras leads his army across a plain in Denmark. He leaves a captain to greet Claudius and get his approval for the march through Danish territory. Hamlet, escorted by Rosencrantz and Guildenstern, appears and questions the captain. He learns that the Norwegian soldiers are about to fight with the Poles over "a little patch of ground" which is practically worthless. Requesting his escort to move ahead, the Prince pauses to reflect upon the implications of what he has just learned. He sees in Fortinbras' determined move against the Poles another reproach of himself. True greatness, he concludes, means to act decisively when honor is the issue. Yet he, whose father has been murdered and whose mother has been morally corrupted, has let time lapse without executing revenge upon Claudius. From now on, his "thoughts [will] be bloody, or be nothing worth" (66).

Commentary

In this scene Hamlet soliloquizes at length for the last time. Some critics have described this soliloquy as Hamlet's most decisive one in that it puts an end to doubt and vacillation. This may be true; but, as much as any passage in the play, it poses problems and raises questions. Once more Hamlet's words often echo what he has said earlier, and they have the curious effect of refuting certain theories confidently advanced by some critics.

"How all occasions do inform against me,/ And spur my dull revenge!" Hamlet begins. What are the "occasions" to which he may be making reference? If he is referring to decisive action in general, the primary example has been provided by Claudius, when he authorized the "lawful espials" of Polonius and of Rosencrantz and Guildenstern, and certainly when he arranged for Hamlet's departure to England, where he would be put to death. They may well include the example of the king-slayer Pyrrhus, who delayed only momentarily, as was made clear in the lines recited by the First Player during the recital of a part of *AEneas and Dido,* which the Prince wished to hear. Both are indeed "Examples gross as earth" (46): the first, devoid of all honor and motivated by criminal ambition and fear; the other, the barbarous execution of personal blood-revenge. The present example, as Hamlet's own words indicate, is no less gross. Surely, no one would wish to see the Prince follow such patterns of action.

Hamlet's comparison of himself to Fortinbras has been widely recognized as thematic, and there are some commentators who insist that the young Norwegian Prince is the most important foil to Hamlet in this play. Like the Prince of Denmark, he has lost a royal father and is intent on executing prompt revenge, for which purpose he has raised his army of "landless resolutes" (I.i.95 ff.). He had planned to invade Denmark. But, thanks to Claudius' diplomatic efforts, the ruler of Norway was persuaded to forego revenge and to expend his martial energy in an attack on Poland (II.ii.65 ff.). It has been argued that Fortinbras, unlike Hamlet, has mastered passion, embraced the dictates of reason, yet does not lapse into inactivity. From this point of view, he does provide a contrast to Hamlet. The difficulty, however, lies in the immediate reason given for Fortinbras' decision to engage the Polish forces. Does Hamlet mean that it is "divine ambition" which makes the Norwegian Prince dare "fortune, death, and danger," knowing that some twenty thousand men probably will be slaughtered—all for the possession of a worthless patch of ground, all for what he deems to be an honorable cause? Surely this cannot be the case, as Hamlet's next lines, properly understood, indicate:

> Rightly to be great
> Is not to stir without great argument
> But greatly to find quarrel in a straw
> When honour's at the stake.
>
> (53-56)

The difficulty of interpretation lies in the phrase "Is not to stir." Perhaps a comma after *Is*, indicating that the "not" belongs with the linking verb rather than with the infinitive would help; otherwise, it appears that the perceptive, intellectual young Hamlet suddenly embraces a very superficial view of honor. The only possible example which Fortinbras provides Hamlet, then, relates to his prompt action, undeterred by thoughts of consequences. Hamlet's own reason for acting—his "quarrel" (argument)—is not in "a straw," nor is the enterprise of vindicating family honor and punishing a fratricide and usurper an "eggshell."

But what of the most impressively philosophical lines in this soliloquy?

> What is a man,
> If his chief good and market of his time
> Be but to sleep and feed? A beast, no more.
> Sure, He that made us with such large discourse,
> Looking before and after, gave us not
> That capability and god-like reason
> To fust in us unus'd.
>
> (33-39)

These lines relate back to Hamlet's "What a piece of work is a man" speech (II.ii.315-19) and amplify what he said then: man is endowed with reason and must put this divine gift to use through positive action. Hamlet goes on to accuse himself of either "Bestial oblivion" (which may be discounted immediately) or "Of thinking too precisely on th' event," arguing that "thought which, quarter'd hath but one part wisdom/And ever three parts coward" (40-43). This is the passage upon which the Romantics, including Goethe and Coleridge, especially depend to justify their concept of Hamlet as the ineffectual dreamer, convinced, it would seem, that his lacerating self-criticism is valid here and elsewhere in the play, rather than providing evidence of his difficulty in subduing passion or of his understandable sense of frustration in view of the obstacles which have prevented him from sweeping to his revenge. It may be argued that "thinking too precisely on th' event" would mean to reject effective reason, and that it is better to have only one-fourth wisdom than to try to solve momentous questions with none at all. If all this be true, then one may conclude that Shakespeare is particularly interested in working toward a precise definition of the moral issue which his tragic hero faces.

And what is to be made of the following lines spoken by Hamlet after he has accused himself of cowardice?

> I do not know
> Why yet I live to say, "This thing's to do,"
> Sith I have cause and will and strength and means
> To do't.
>
> (43-46)

This is exactly the temper of the Hamlet who soliloquized "O, what a rogue and peasant slave am I!" and of the Hamlet of the "To be, or not to be" soliloquy. In the brief time that has elapsed since he sprang the Mouse-trap, Hamlet has had one real opportunity to kill Claudius, but he does know *why* he failed to do so. Understandably, some commentators suggest that this soliloquy has been misplaced; but it is more logical to conclude that the Prince has been emotionally aroused by just what he says — one more "occasion" reminding him that after many months the murderer-usurper survives and rules Denmark with Gertrude as his "imperial jointress."

"O, from this time forth,/My thoughts be bloody, or be nothing worth!" the Prince concludes. His thoughts were sufficiently bloody when he spoke the lines of his second soliloquy, and certainly when he came upon the kneeling Claudius shortly after he had sprung the Mouse-trap and caught the conscience of the King. Perhaps Fortinbras' single-minded pursuit of his goal has provided Hamlet with an example, however gross, which will make it possible for him to act positively and promptly if an opportunity presents itself. So full of self-reproach is he now that apparently the end will justify whatever means he can find. In part, such a conclusion is supported by the fact that this scene leads to the final, larger movement in the play, one in which the tragic hero no longer will have the need to express his doubts and his perplexities.

ACT IV – SCENE 5

Summary

A court gentleman informs Gertrude that Ophelia seems to be out of her mind and in her pitiable state has become troublesome. Gertrude flatly states that she will not see her. When the gentleman tells how Ophelia speaks constantly of her father and behaves in a most erratic manner, Horatio points out that her wild discourse may arouse suspicion. Gertrude then agrees to see her.

Ophelia enters, asks for "the beauteous majesty of Denmark," talks incoherently, and sings verses of ballads, one obviously relating thematically to the death of her elderly father, the other two relating to the seduction of an innocent maiden. Claudius, who has joined the group, addresses her graciously but receives no rational reply. He is convinced that her father's death has driven her mad. When she leaves, he orders that she be closely watched. He then turns to Gertrude, summarizes the troubles in Elsinore: Polonius slain; Hamlet no longer in the kingdom; the body of the Lord Chamberlain hastily and secretly buried; the King's subjects suspicious and increasingly restless; Laertes, returned in secret from France, being incited by unwholesome rumors. Claudius is in a state of torment.

Loud noises are heard, and the King calls for his Switzers (mercenary soldiers) to guard the door, just as a messenger enters to report that Laertes and a mob who hail him as Claudius' successor have overcome officers of the guard and are about to break in. That is exactly what happens. But Laertes orders his followers to take up a position outside the room and then addresses the King and Queen, demanding that they "give" him his father. Gertrude urges him to calm down, but it is the politic Claudius who succeeds in reasoning with the distraught Laertes.

Ophelia returns, again singing snatches of a ballad, the words of which relate to the sad death of a man with "beard as white as snow," and again talking incoherently. In fantasy, she distributes various flowers to those who watch and listen to her. Laertes is beside himself with grief for his "kind sister, sweet Ophelia." When Ophelia leaves, Claudius succeeds in getting Laertes' attention. He promises to join Laertes in punishing the guilty in the matter of Polonius' death.

Commentary

The irony in this scene is quite striking. Ophelia has spoken of Hamlet's mind as being "o'erthrown" (III.i.158), but it is she who is now mad. Some have raised the question of whether her madness, so distressing since she has been no more than the dutiful daughter of a vain and foolish father, is necessary to the plot. One critic, for example, argues that Laertes has motive enough to act as he does without his sister's madness, which he calls a "dramatic luxury" (L. L. Schücking, *Character Problems in Shakespeare's Plays,* 1922, p. 172). Further, if one is convinced that Hamlet should have left Claudius, as well as Gertrude, to heaven (in which case the Ghost is an evil spirit intent on leading Hamlet to his destruction), Ophelia's madness and subsequent death result from "the frightening process of a course that never should have been initiated" (E. Prosser, p. 212). The consensus is that Ophelia's madness and death have a logical place in the entire action because they coincide with, and illustrate, one result of disorder in the State – the rottenness which has been spreading through the body politic.

The second tragic love song sung by Ophelia, beginning with "To-morrow is Saint Valentine's day" and concluding with "An thou hadst not come to my bed," has intrigued many commentators. Those who read the play primarily as a romantic love tragedy involving Hamlet and Ophelia recall that Ophelia has already spoken of having "suck'd the honey of his music vows" (III.i.164) and are convinced that Hamlet has had his way with Ophelia and then rejected her. For some of these romantics, this is the primary cause of her mental collapse, the death of her father being the secondary cause. They have at least the virtue of consistency when they come to the next scene, where Ophelia's death by drowning is reported: the young lady, it seems, drowned herself because, to her disgrace, she was carrying Hamlet's child! Like Polonius, when he first learned that the Prince was paying attention to his daughter, this group of interpretators believe that Hamlet did not have honorable intentions. This is obviously the *reductio ad absurdum* of impressionism.

What is the justification for having Ophelia sing a song, the theme of which is the seduction and abandonment of an innocent maiden? It will be recalled that the suspicious Polonius had instructed his daughter not to be so naive as to think that the Prince would marry her – not to be misled by Hamlet's importuning her in what she reported as "honourable fashion"; he ordered her to spend no more time in Hamlet's company (I.iii.126 ff.). Thereafter she sought him out only when directed to do so by Polonius, who ignored the Prince's warning that

"Conception is a blessing, but not as [his] daughter may conceive" (II.ii.185-87), an indication that Hamlet was fully aware that Ophelia had reported to her father how he had appeared to her when he first adopted the antic disposition. The ambiguity in Hamlet's later injunction, "Get thee to a nunnery, go" (III.i.142), made clear (as has been pointed out) that he was aware of her personal innocence and, at the same time, knew that she had been "loosed" upon him. Earlier, in his third long soliloquy, he spoke bitterly of the "pangs of dispriz'd love" (III.i.72), and in the shenting scene, he told Gertrude that her marriage to Claudius was

> Such an act
> That blurs the grace and blush of modesty,
> Calls virtue hypocrite, takes off the rose
> From the fair forehead of an innocent love
> And sets a blister there. . . .
>
> (III.iv.40-44)

In the commentary, the implications of this speech and especially its application to the unfortunate Ophelia were emphasized. Further, it has been pointed out that illicit sex in Shakespeare's later dramas is repeatedly used as a symbol of pervading evil. All this adds up to one conclusion: Ophelia's song is intended to underscore the destructive force of evil in the kingdom. And the source of the infection is Claudius, murderer and usurper, who has won over the weak Gertrude to an incestuous marriage, encouraged the underhanded activities of his old Lord Chamberlain, and now has arranged for the murder of Hamlet. Ophelia is the latest victim; little wonder, then, that she should sing of "dispriz'd love." Nor is this conclusion inconsistent with the claim that Hamlet's harsh words to her in the nunnery scene planted the image of illicit sex in her mind.

Ophelia's distribution of the flowers (perhaps imaginary, although her first words in the First Quarto after her return are "Wel God a mercy, I a bin gathering of floures.") is of some interest in terms of symbolism. To her brother she gives rosemary, which was used at both weddings and funerals as a symbol of remembrance. It may be her impending death, not just that of Polonius, that is symbolized here; if so, her words indeed comprise "A document [piece of instruction] in madness," as Laertes says (178). Pansies, which she also gives to Laertes, symbolize thoughts, and therefore are no less appropriate. Apparently the fennel, representing flattery, is given to the King, and the columbines, symbolizing thanklessness, to the Queen. To Gertrude also are given the rue and daisy, the first ("herb of grace") symbolizes sorrow, and the second may represent a warning to women who are too easily persuaded to love. Neither Gertrude nor Claudius is given violets, which stand for faithfulness—but perhaps Ophelia's words explaining why she cannot distribute the violets are addressed to Horatio.

In this scene, it is Laertes who emerges as a foil to Hamlet. He has been stirred by "great argument," to use the phrase from the Prince's last soliloquy. Like Hamlet, he has lost a beloved father, one who was slain. When the Ghost concluded its account of King Hamlet's murder, it had called upon Hamlet to prove that he had "nature" (natural feelings) in him by avenging his father's death (I.v.81). There is no question regarding such nature in Laertes, who is not to be restrained in his determination to prove that he is his father's son. Laertes is "stirred" to vindicate the honor of his family. After the news of his father's death reached him in Paris, he left for Elsinore; now he has burst into the room and threatens the King. Laertes, it would seem, is the model avenger for a tragedy of blood. He will act first and act promptly, undeterred by questions of public duty, morality, or consequences:

> I dare damnation. To this point I stand,
> That both the worlds I give to negligence,
> Let come what comes; only I'll be reveng'd
> Most throughly for my father.
>
> (133-36)

There is little danger of conscience making a coward of Laertes or of his thinking too precisely on the event. In his own way, he is as single-minded as Fortinbras, who is determined to fight over "a little patch of ground," whatever the cost in human lives may be.

When Laertes first sees Ophelia, now deranged, the dramatic poignancy of the meeting is not to be denied. Yet his speech (154-63) beginning "O heat, dry up my brains!" is sufficiently overwrought and artificial in style to suggest that the player describing the grief of Hecuba might well have recited it. Perhaps all this may seem to be too harsh a criticism of a youth who loved and was loyal to the members of his family, one who was especially concerned that his father had been denied proper burial and honors appropriate for a Lord Chamberlain (See lines 212-17). But the point is that, although he too may serve as a foil to Hamlet, he is anything but a norm character. If there has been an excess evident in the Prince's lines, it has been present only when he soliloquizes.

Before leaving the discussion of Laertes in this scene, one should call attention to the fact that he was able to raise a rebellion of sorts. It is reasonable to ask why Hamlet, whose popularity was established by the testimony of Ophelia (III.i.159 ff.) and that of Claudius (IV.iii.4), did not secure public support in a revolt against the King. Some have believed that he could have done so, succeeded in deposing Claudius, and even had the usurper brought to trial for regicide. All this, of course, would have entailed a drastic revision of the original story elements.

Moreover, in Shakespeare's play, evidence of political discontent, of disorder in the body politic, has been presented only subsequent to the death of Polonius.

Close attention to the lines spoken by Claudius makes clear how intense the conflict in this play has become. "O Gertrude, Gertrude," says the guilt-ridden King, "When sorrows come, they come not single spies,/ But in battalions" (77-79). Of course he is striving to sustain the public image of a virtuous ruler and concerned kinsman of a Prince who, in his madness, has disrupted an orderly realm. Actually Claudius is an increasingly fearful individual. But he remains a strong adversary; there is no danger that he will collapse or suddenly abandon the conflict. He is still the adroit Machiavellian, gifted in dissembling and prompt in action. In this role, Claudius achieves supreme irony when he speaks sententiously of "poor Ophelia" (85-87) and when he urges Gertrude not to restrain the enraged Laertes, mouthing orthodox Renaissance political doctrine:

> Let him go, Gertrude; do not fear our person.
> There's such divinity doth hedge a king
> That treason can but peep to what it would.
>
> (121-23)

This is the public image of a ruler which the competent Claudius has presented, although one may agree with Hamlet that he is actually "a king of shreds and patches." No one is likely to underestimate his skill when he succeeds in quelling Laertes' wrath, assuring the Lord Chamberlain's son that, if he (Claudius) is found to be to blame in any degree, he will forfeit both kingdom and life (203-9), and promising that Laertes will be given complete satisfaction: "And where the offence is let the great axe fall" (218). When one comes to the final scene, the resolution of this tragedy, these words will be recognized as ironic; but immediately they reveal the King not only saving himself from the immediate threat posed by Laertes' revolt, but also capitalizing upon that very turn of events. If Hamlet is put to death in accordance with Claudius' instructions, the members of the Court and, one may assume, the public at large, convinced by Claudius that he has become a homicidal maniac, will not be "Thick and unwholesome in their thoughts and whispers," to use the King's own words (82).

There remains something to be said about Gertrude in this scene. Once more she exhibits passive compliance in her relationship with Claudius, but there is more to be said about her. Although she sincerely believes that her son is mentally ill, she too suffers from the "unquiet mind" of the mortal sinner.

ACT IV – SCENE 6

Summary

Horatio is told by his attendant that some sailors wish to give him certain letters. Aware that he knows of no one except Hamlet who might have written to him, he immediately instructs the attendant to let the sailors enter. From the letter, Horatio learns that the ship bearing Hamlet to England was attacked by pirates. During the engagement, Hamlet boarded the pirate ship and was made captive. He has been well treated and brought back to Denmark in return for his promise to do them a good turn. Horatio is to deliver the other letters to the King and then come to Hamlet without delay, for he has much to tell his friend. Horatio promises to reward the sailors when they have guided him to the Prince.

Commentary

The sailors, it is sufficiently clear, are some of the pirates who detained Hamlet and then returned him to Denmark. The return of Hamlet is a plain indication that the resolution of the entire action is not far off.

ACT IV – SCENE 7

Summary

The King has told Laertes that Hamlet killed Polonius and sought to kill him, Claudius. When Laertes asks why the King did not apprehend the Prince and have him punished for such capital offences, Claudius explains that he did not do so for two reasons: first, the Queen dotes upon her son and, devoted as he is to her, he restrained himself; second, he could not expect support from the public, who reveres Hamlet. He assures Laertes that he has never considered letting the Prince escape punishment, about which Laertes will hear more.

At this point a messenger enters with letters from Hamlet, one for the King and one for the Queen. From his letter, Claudius learns that the Prince has returned to Denmark. Immediately the King proceeds to engage Laertes in a plot to kill Hamlet. The King tells him how Hamlet's sense of rivalry was aroused by the report of Laertes' skill in fencing. Laertes, he says, can prove that he loved his father by taking advantage of this situation as a means of avenging Polonius' death without risking injury to himself. When Laertes declares that nothing could restrain him from acting against Hamlet, Claudius tells him that he will arrange a fencing match between the two and that Laertes will use a foil with an unblunted point. Laertes than can kill Hamlet before the eyes of the spectators without appearing to intend any harm to his adversary. Laertes not only agrees but plans to go beyond this: he will dip the point of his rapier in deadly poison. Claudius adds a second means of insuring Hamlet's death. He will have prepared, and available, a cup of poisoned wine for Hamlet to drink if Laertes somehow fails to draw blood in the duel.

Gertrude enters, lamenting. She informs Laertes that his sister is drowned. Both he and Claudius learn that, while Ophelia was weaving fantastic garlands and hanging them on the limbs of a willow tree, a limb broke and she fell into the stream. For a brief time she had floated, then she sank to her death. Laertes strives to control his grief but cannot do so. Nor can he speak the fiery words he had intended to address to Claudius. When he leaves, Claudius tells Gertrude that now he must begin once more the task of calming Laertes' rage.

Commentary

Repeatedly, Claudius has been described as Machiavellian in his villainy. But it also has been pointed out that, unlike the usual Machiavellian villain of the Elizabethan stage, he suffers the pangs of conscience and is not the heartless diabolist who scoffs at religion and gloats over his own wickedness. As one definitely learns in this scene, he is genuinely fond of Gertrude; and this capacity for love is another characteristic which differentiates him from the completely dedicated Machiavellian. In other respects — cunning, capacity for cruelty, sagacity however misdirected, adeptness at improvision — Claudius, especially in this scene, can take his place at the side of Richard III, Iago, Edmund, and other stage villains who in many ways, if not all, are Machiavellian types.

In winning over Laertes, the last and most formidable agent he uses against Hamlet, Claudius succeeds in presenting himself as a ruler who has failed to act for a reason which tends to reflect favorably upon his character. Although he acknowledges the fact that his nephew is popular, he is astute enough not to mention that, as he had said in an earlier scene, the Prince is "lov'd by the distracted multitude." It is also characteristic of him that he should formulate a plan which, if executed properly, will not involve much risk:

> And for his death no wind of blame shall breathe,
> But even his mother shall uncharge the practice
> And call it accident.

(67-69)

This, of course, is the practical, the politic way in which "Diseases desperate grown" are relieved in a world where "seeming" and "acting" are a way of life. To use Polonius' words spoken to Reynaldo, it is the way employed by those of "wisdom and of reach" (II.i.64). There is, then, a certain logic, even inevitability, in the choice of poison for the purpose of killing Hamlet: it was poison which Claudius used to gain his crown and wife; poison began the whole process of this villainy.

Claudius' Machiavellianism is evident not only in his prompt approval of Laertes' plan to use a foil tipped with poison, but also in planning to have the poisoned drink ready, should Laertes fail. To some extent, it is also evident in his report that the Norman horseman had the highest praise for Laertes' skill in swordsmanship and that Hamlet became envious when he heard Laertes praised. And so when, having learned that Hamlet has returned to Denmark alone and "naked" (unarmed), Claudius asks Laertes: "Can you advise me?" (54). Perhaps Claudius knows very well that modesty is not a notable trait in Polonius' son and certainly he knows that flattery can be an effective device.

Laertes remains the "perfect" revenger, one not to be deterred by anything, just as in Act IV, Scene vi, when he burst into the room and confronted Claudius. But now there is a great falling off in his character. Whatever his limitations may have been heretofore, he invited great sympathy. His cause was great: a father slain and denied a decent funeral, his sister driven mad. It is not just that he is easily won over by Claudius; to decide on that basis that he is quite naive is to underestimate the formidability of Hamlet's adversary. Rather it is that he is the one who, even prior to listening to Claudius' plan, intended to use a rapier with a poisoned tip. One can only conclude that he is his father's son and cannot be wholly aboveboard. But the issue now is one of life and death. Admittedly, Laertes recovers one's sympathy after he learns of Ophelia's death, especially because, in contrast to the ranting style he used when he saw and heard his demented sister in Act IV, Scene v, he now speaks moving words and is impressively restrained (186-92). Nevertheless, it is this report of Ophelia's death that seals the pact between Laertes and Claudius.

Unlike Hamlet, neither Claudius nor Laertes can be charged with dullness or delay; both intend to act promptly and decisively. In a sense, these two provide another "occasion" which Hamlet might well see as one which informs against him. And, although Laertes has shown himself to be voluble enough, from the moment of his return to Denmark he has been acting positively, motivated by the single intention of avenging his father's death. Conscience will not make him a coward; he stands ready to cut Hamlet's throat in the church.

When Claudius asks Laertes if his father was dear to him (108), one recalls the Ghost's words to Hamlet: "If thou didst ever thy dear father

love—" and its command that Hamlet prove his love: "Revenge his foul
and most unnatural murder" (I.v.23-25). Audience and reader alike are
forcibly reminded that the Prince has delayed; months have elapsed,
yet Claudius survives as King of Denmark. Among those who go far
toward accepting Hamlet's self-indictment for not sweeping to his revenge (the victim of excessive grief), this entire episode is called upon
to support their interpretation. It would seem more reasonable to conclude that throughout this scene, in which he does not appear, Hamlet
emerges as the admirable tragic hero, despite delays and alleged ration-
alizations for them. Claudius acknowledges him to be "Most generous
and free from all contriving" (136). It follows that, although procrastination made possible what has been called the "increase in the area of
destruction," the Prince himself is the sacrificial victim of his superior
morality: his very virtues work to his disadvantage in the corrupt world
in which he finds himself. Laertes surely could use considerable "thinking . . . precisely on th' event," the propensity for which Hamlet felt
might be the cause of his failure to carry out the Ghost's injunction
(IV.iv.41). And when Laertes declares his willingness to cut Hamlet's
throat in the church, he obviously could use some of Hamlet's moral
scrupulousness. But even here, it may be pointed out (if only to demonstrate the difficulties which this play poses) that when Laertes makes
his wild statement, one is reminded of Hamlet's refusal to kill Claudius
as the latter knelt for prayer. One also recalls that the Prince was motivated not by religious compunction but by a determination to obtain
"perfect" revenge. Yet, in the balance, the Prince of Denmark emerges
as admirable. He could no more seek to avenge his father's death in the
way adopted by Laertes than he could emulate Fortinbras in leading
troops to slaughter for the sake of a worthless patch of ground, despite
his generalization regarding what constitutes true greatness when
honor is the issue. Although his slaying of Polonius was the result of
an impulsive action, he had lamented the fact that he should have been
called upon to be either minister or scourge.

"One woe doth tread upon another's heel,/ So fast they follow,"
says the distraught Gertrude (164), and Ophelia's sad death by drowning is revealed. One recalls Claudius' words of despair when he witnessed her madness:

> O Gertrude, Gertrude,
> When sorrows come, they come not single spies,
> But in battalions.
>
> (IV.v.77-79)

The rottenness in the state of Denmark, present from the beginning of
this play, has spread. The tragic course of events has been gaining

increasing momentum and has reached this crucial point at the end of Act IV. Gertrude's highly lyrical and touching description of Ophelia's death is a set-piece. That it is appropriate to the Queen has been questioned; but the Gertrude who has emerged as genuinely devoted to her son surely is capable of sincere grief for the death of Ophelia. More relevant is the fact that, from Gertrude's report, it is clear that Ophelia's death was accidental, not suicide, a fact that poses a minor problem in view of the disputation in the next scene regarding her burial.

ACT V – SCENE 1

Summary

Two gravediggers discuss the recent inquest of the death of Ophelia, held to determine whether or not she was a suicide and, concomitantly, whether or not she merits a Christian burial. The First Gravedigger is convinced that she will be accorded that privilege only because she is a gentlewoman. In the grimly comic dialogue which follows, the two identify themselves with Adam, the "first gentleman" and the first delver, and then with the gallows-maker, who builds a frame that outlives its tenants.

While the Second Gravedigger goes to fetch a pot of liquor, Hamlet and Horatio enter, pausing to listen to the First Gravedigger as he sings snatches of a ballad and digs in the earth. When he tosses up a skull and dashes it to the ground, the Prince is impelled to muse upon death as the great leveler of all people. He then questions the First Gravedigger, who answers him in chop-logic, a particular kind of dialectical speech in which the practitioner insists upon confining himself to a special meaning of a given word or phrase. In reply to a question, the gravedigger states that he has followed his calling since the day when King Hamlet defeated old King Fortinbras of Norway, on which day young Hamlet ("he that was mad, and sent into England") was born — thirty years ago, so he says.

Hamlet questions him further. The gravedigger identifies the skull as that of Yorick, the King's jester, who died twenty-three years ago. Hamlet picks it up and tells Horatio that Yorick was his childhood favorite. Now once more he dwells upon death, which brings not only a court jester to this state but also the vain court lady and even great conquerors like Alexander the Great and Caesar, whose dust may now fill a bunghole or a chink in a wall.

As the funeral procession enters, the members of which include the King, the Queen, and Laertes, Hamlet and Horatio step back, unobserved. Laertes complains to the Priest about the limited rites accorded his dead sister. The surly Priest insists that Ophelia is being accorded obsequies which she really does not deserve in view of the doubtful circumstances of her death.

When Ophelia's body is lowered into the grave, the Queen strews the coffin with flowers and speaks touchingly of her defeated hope that Ophelia would have become Hamlet's wife. Laertes, no longer able to restrain himself, cries out in grief and then leaps into the grave, asking that he be buried with his sister. At this point in the action, Hamlet steps forth and demands to know why Laertes should so emphasize his sorrow. Announcing himself as "Hamlet, the Dane," he too leaps into the grave. Laertes seizes him by the throat, and the two grapple until they are separated by attendants and then climb out of the grave.

Horatio attempts to calm the Prince, but the latter is not to be silenced. He declares that he loved Ophelia far more than Laertes could have loved her, bitterly criticizes Laertes for indulging in bombast, and then insists that he has always held him in high esteem. Gertrude again expresses her belief that her son is mad. After Hamlet leaves, Claudius speaks to Laertes, reminding him that he has not long to wait for vengeance.

Commentary

In the first act, Claudius, addressing the assembled Court, had spoken of "mirth in funeral" and "delight and dole" (I.ii.12-13). His words well express the theme of the first part of this scene. The gravediggers are identified as "two clowns"; that is, they are lowly (and often rustic) characters who will provide broad comedy in the midst of tragic action. It should be apparent that the comic element in this scene has comparable relevancy. Moreover, the First Gravedigger, so far as his gift for paradox is concerned, has at his level and, in his way, a certain affinity with Hamlet himself when the Prince chooses to exercise his sardonic wit. However brief his appearance may be in this play, the First Gravedigger is a memorable figure.

More often than not, incongruity is basic to comedy. For these two lowly gravediggers to discuss with such intensity a profound theological and legal question, and especially to hear the first one endeavor to introduce into his argument technical Latinisms and to organize his argument in strict accordance with the rules of Aristotelian logic, with its careful definition of a key term—all this is wonderful comedy of words. Inevitably, the malapropism finds a place. Instead of *se defendendo* (in self-defense), the First Gravedigger says *se offendendo,* and he renders the Latin *ergo* (therefore) as *argal.* In what amounts to a burlesque of the scholastic method of disputation, he defines the "three branches" of an act, with a resulting redundancy that is hilarious. The two are no less amusing when the transition is made to Adam, the first delver and the progenitor of the human race – proof that the gravediggers, like gardeners and ditch-diggers, are descendents of the first human being, who was a gentleman (Could Adam delve without arms?). Shakespeare and all members of his audience were familiar with the traditional doggerel:

> When Adam delved and Eve span,
> Who was then the gentleman?

The underlying note of social protest gives way to grim humor when the First Gravedigger proposes his riddle – indeed, the ultimate riddle: "What is he that builds stronger than either the mason, the shipwright, or the carpenter?" (46-47). His fellow gravedigger is praised for the case he makes in favor of the gallows-maker (that specialist among carpenters), but he proves to be too obtuse to hit the obvious answers.

Few can miss the underlying seriousness in much of this buffoonery. If nothing else, it serves to emphasize the Christian framework of *Hamlet* and to remind one that Hamlet himself is a Christian Prince who has been called upon to execute revenge. Ophelia's guilt, if any, depends upon whether or not her drowning was a voluntary act. If it was voluntary, obviously she was guilty of self-murder. Other lives have been taken in the course of the action, including that of Polonius; others soon will be lost – and not just the life of Hamlet's adversary. The Prince has been, and will be, involved in most of these deaths. What, if any, is the extent of his guilt? In all instances does he, and will he, function as the righteous minister of God's justice or as a scourge? These are proper questions, although neither takes into consideration the special difficulties posed by the corruption prevalent in Denmark and the element of chance.

The gravediggers' dialogue, with its emphasis largely on death, also serves as a prologue to the "worm's meat" or "Dance of Death" theme developed in this same scene by Hamlet. Perhaps there is even relevancy in the song which the First Gravedigger sings, a conventional Tudor one in which youth and age are contrasted. Admittedly, it may do no more than show some feeling on the part of the singer, despite Hamlet's question, "Has this fellow no feeling of his business that he sings at grave-making?" (73-74). But youth and age are not the only subjects of the song; love and renunciation are also contrasted. Time is the destroyer of youth, inevitably; but it can also destroy love. And this too looks forward to the subject of Hamlet's morbid remarks.

When Hamlet sees the First Gravedigger toss up the skulls, he exclaims: "How the knave jowls it to the ground, as if it were Cain's jawbone, that did the first murder!" (84-85). Since Cain's crime was fratricide, the special import of this exclamation is evident. One recalls Claudius' words, spoken in soliloquy, after the Mouse-trap had been sprung:

> O, my offence is rank, it smells to heaven;
> It hath the primal eldest curse upon't,
> A brother's murder.
>
> (III.iii.36-38)

Carried along by his satirical imagination and universalizing tendencies, Hamlet meditates on the ironical fact that overreaching politicians, lawyers with all their tricks, self-seeking courtiers, vain court ladies, even those held to be exemplars of greatness in this world ultimately are no more than the "quintessence of dust." Among the examples of earthly vanity which he adduces, the following is the culminating one:

> Now get you to my lady's chamber,
> and tell her, let her paint an inch thick, to this
> favour she must come. Make her laugh at that.
>
> (212-14)

It is quite possible that more than human vanity is involved here. In two significant, earlier passages, comparable references to woman's efforts at beautification were used to exemplify hypocrisy or dishonesty in general. The first was included in the King's aside after he heard Polonius instruct Ophelia on how to conduct herself once she was "loosed" upon Hamlet:

> The harlot's cheek, beautified with plast'ring art,
> Is not more ugly to the thing that helps it
> Than is my deed to my most painted word.
>
> (III.i.51-53)

The second reference was part of Hamlet's bitter indictment of Ophelia in the nunnery scene:

> I have heard of your paintings too, well enough.
> God has given you one face, and you make yourself
> another.
>
> (III.i.148-50)

The conclusion to be drawn, then, is that Hamlet's discourse is not just another example of morbid preoccupation with death, amounting to what some insist is a death wish; nor is it a premonition of his own impending death. Rather, it underscores once more, and this late in the play, the extent of his disillusionment. Were he to sweep to his revenge and survive to rule Denmark, Hamlet's outlook on life could never be the optimistic one which once made it possible for him to embrace the idealistic Renaissance view of man as the paragon of animals, like unto the angels.

All this provides a transition to the puzzling remarks which the First Gravedigger makes to Hamlet. From his words, one learns that he began his career on the very day Hamlet was born (160-61) and has served for thirty years (177). A thirty-year-old Hamlet, undergraduate at Wittenberg? One who apparently was not considered as eligible to succeed his father because of his youth? This has been and remains a crux. It has been argued that the Hamlet whom one meets in Act V has experienced so much that he is no longer the youth who, overwhelmed not only by the sudden death of a beloved father but more especially by the hasty and incestuous marriage of his mother, wishes for death. Such an impressionistic theory would be consistent with much that has been written about Hamlet's development of the "worm's meat" theme in this play. But there have been other conjectures about Hamlet's age as reported by the First Gravedigger. It has been pointed out correctly that Shakespeare was not always careful about exact details, either those relating to chronology or those relating to topography. Further, the Elizabethans not infrequently made use of round numbers, the implication here being that the Gravedigger means that he had followed his vocation for somewhat more than twenty years. Finally, there are those who believe that in this passage Shakespeare inadvertently included a detail peculiar to an earlier version of the Hamlet story. One other theory may well be added to these: Hamlet suddenly emerges as a man of thirty years, thanks to a careless transcriber or printer. Most Shakespeareans refuse to trouble themselves greatly over this detail, convinced that the poet-dramatist intended his tragic hero to be the gifted son of King Hamlet put to the test not in his adult maturity but at his inception to manhood. The student may well look to the end of the play and read Fortinbras' encomium. The Norwegian Prince's words could hardly refer to an individual who had been a promising young man for a decade or more.

The discussion of Ophelia's burial, in which the Priest and Laertes take part, calls for some commentary. The Priest's insistence that "Her death was doubtful" (250) is at variance with Gertrude's report of accidental death in the preceding scene. One learns that Ophelia is to be buried in sanctified ground only because "great command o'ersways the order" (251), an indication that the King himself interceded after the coroner's verdict. It is established, however, that the pathetic Ophelia died chaste and therefore is allowed "virgin rites" (255). Not without interest also is the fact that once more she is associated with flowers. "Lay her i' th' earth," Laertes exclaims in anguish, "And from her fair and unpolluted flesh/May violets spring!" (261-62). Gertrude, who appears most sympathetic in this scene, scatters flowers on the coffin and says, "Sweets to the sweet; farewell!" (266). When Ophelia first appeared in this play she was associated with flowers and specifically with the violet, a symbol of faithfulness, but also a flower which is "sweet, not lasting"; she was associated also with other "infants of the spring" (I.iii.7-8, 39-40). Much later in the play, a demented Ophelia distributed flowers among the members of the Court group, but these did not include violets, for they had withered when her father died (IV.vi.179-85). All this adds up to a sufficiently obvious conclusion: Ophelia metaphorically is the flower destroyed by "Contagious blastments," to use Laertes' words (I.iii.42), in a Denmark ruled by a usurper and regicide who lives in incestuous union with his queen.

It may come as something of a surprise to find the Queen saying, as she scatters flowers on Ophelia's coffin,

> I hop'd thou shouldst have been my Hamlet's wife.
> I thought thy bride-bed to have deck'd, sweet maid,
> And not t' have strew'd thy grave.
>
> (267-69)

One recalls that both Laertes (I.iii.14-21) and Polonius (I.iv.123-30) rejected the idea that Hamlet might marry Ophelia, the former arguing that the Prince would have to have a political marriage, the latter, typically refusing to believe that Hamlet could have honorable intentions. The Queen's words make all the more pathetic the death of Ophelia and show how destructive the force of evil has been up to this point, late in the play. Those who read into *Hamlet* romantic love as the primary element make much of Gertrude's words, just as they do Hamlet's declaration that he loved Ophelia more than forty thousand times as much as brother could love sister (292-93). But when one stays with the text, he knows that love between Hamlet and Ophelia has been excluded from the very first; Hamlet can speak of it only when she is dead. The Prince returned to Elsinore only when he learned of his father's death. Both Laertes and Polonius spoke of the *recent* attentions Hamlet paid to Ophelia. There are two possibilities: first, he did love her deeply prior to his mother's marriage to Claudius, which took place less than two months after his father's funeral, and then was repulsed by the conviction that she had deserted him; second, he had turned to her originally to test the validity of his own generalization voiced in his first soliloquy: "Frailty, thy name is woman!" If the latter be true, then one may well conclude that his declaration of boundless love for Ophelia is to be interpreted as an expression of his shock at, and genuine sorrow for, the death of Ophelia, whose only possible offense was that she was obedient to a father who was a rash, intruding fool.

Overlapping the problem of interpretation here and adding to the complexity are the performances of Laertes and Hamlet. As the funeral procession arrives, the Prince speaks of Laertes to Horatio: "That is Laertes, a very noble youth" (247), an inadvertently ironic remark in view of what has been revealed about Laertes. One hardly equates nobility with the kind of underhanded scheming revealed in the last scene of Act IV. Is it possible that Hamlet's gracious tribute is intended as a hint for evaluating Laertes' words and actions which soon follow and, to some extent, make understandable Hamlet's reaction?

To be sure, Laertes invites great sympathy, just as he did when he and his sister said their farewells early in the play. But, it has been argued, his advice to Ophelia in that early scene was notable for its affected style; it was anything but natural and spontaneous. Consider also the Laertes whose rebellion had, in Claudius' words, looked so "giant-like" and who was willing to "dare damnation," even if he had to slit an adversary's throat in the church (IV.v.121, 133; vii,127). Now, in the present scene, his rhetorical outburst, followed by his leap into the grave, is so excessive that he appears to be overacting the role of the grief-stricken brother, his expression of grief exceeding that of Hecuba, as described in the player's lines from *Aeneas and Dido*. If this be true, then Hamlet's violent reaction is completely understandable, and especially so when one recalls how he had urged the players to avoid overacting and rant and "to hold . . . the mirror up to nature" (III.ii.22-38). The Prince's own words provide the soundest criticism of Laertes' performance:

> What is he whose grief
> Bears such an emphasis, whose phrase of sorrow
> Conjures the wand'ring stars and makes them stand
> Like wonder-wounded hearers?
>
> (277-80)

After the two are separated, he speaks the lines which are completely devastating, beginning,

> Woo 't weep? Woo 't fight? Woo 't fast?
> Woo 't tear thyself?
> Woo 't drink up eisel [vinegar]? Eat a crocodile?

and concluding, "Nay, an thou'lt mouth, I'll rant as well as thou" (298-307). "Woo 't" was a form used only by illiterates and therefore is intended to be insulting, as are all the elements of competitive hyperbole which follow. If Hamlet has spoken "wild and whirling words" in a state of high excitement, as when he first encountered the Ghost, if he could voice the bitterest words of self-criticism, as he has done in soliloquy on two notable occasions, he is incapable of "mouthing," of "rant." It simply will not do to say, as the neo-Freudians do, that Hamlet's lines are a manifestation of overemphasis resulting from a bad conscience.

"This is I, Hamlet, the Dane!" the Prince exclaims when he moves out from his place of retirement where he has been observing what takes place (280-81). In these words he takes on his father's title. Is he now a Prince who, after indulging himself in meditations, or permitting himself to be engulfed in excessive grief, now speaks with an absolute authority which indicates that he will no longer procrastinate? So some have argued, reasoning that his experience on the voyage to England and the shock of learning that Ophelia is dead have effected this change in his character. Certainly Hamlet no longer is willing to tolerate "seeming" and "acting," any more than he was willing to tolerate the actions of Rosencrantz and Guildenstern, the King's agents. When Laertes grasps him by the throat, he speaks words which are at once decisive and controlled:

> I prithee, take thy fingers from my throat.
> Sir, though I am not splentive [hot-tempered] and rash,
> Yet have I something in me dangerous,
> Which let thy wiseness fear. Away thy hand!
>
> (283-86)

Yet there remain perplexing questions. "What is the reason that you use me thus?" he asks (312). Can Hamlet possibly have forgotten that he has slain Laertes' father? May he not have suspected at least some connection between Polonius' death and that of Ophelia? One readily may discount Gertrude's statement that Hamlet's words and actions comprise evidence of his madness, following which "His silence will sit drooping" (307-11); but Hamlet's last two lines at least suggest that he may have put on the antic disposition for the last time:

> Let Hercules himself do what he may,
> The cat will mew and dog will have his day.
>
> (314-15)

ACT V – SCENE 2

Summary

Hamlet now has the time and the opportunity to tell Horatio all that he experienced since he embarked with Rosencrantz and Guildenstern for England. During the first night at sea, he roused himself, sought out the quarters occupied by the King's agents, and took the sealed packet containing Claudius' instructions to the English king. Thus he discovered that Claudius had ordered that he be beheaded. Immediately Hamlet devised new instructions in the official style requesting that

Claudius' servants who brought the communication to the King of England be put to death. The Prince folded these instructions, placed them in the packet, which he sealed, making use of his father's signet. Then he replaced the packet. On the next day, the sea-fight with the pirates took place, as Hamlet informed Horatio in his letter. Only Hamlet was taken captive; the others proceeded on the voyage to England.

Horatio is appalled to learn the extent of Claudius' villainy, and Hamlet points out that he righteously could slay the man who has killed his royal father, whored his mother, and prevented him from succeeding to the throne. Horatio points out that Claudius will soon learn what has happened to Rosencrantz and Guildenstern, but Hamlet replies that the interim, short though it will be, belongs to him.

Osric, an emissary from the King, enters. Hamlet promptly recognizes him as the affected, overly polite courtier in the service of Claudius. Sardonically, the Prince adopts the same stilted style employed by this "water-fly" and, with a straight face, asks questions and makes comments intended to make Osric exhaust himself in artificial expression. But at last the message is conveyed: Hamlet is challenged to a friendly duel with Laertes, the match to take place before the King and Queen and their attendants. Osric informs the Prince that Claudius is confident that he will excel Laertes in swordsmanship. Hamlet declares that he will win for the King's sake if he can. Osric departs, leaving Hamlet and Horatio to remark on how ridiculous he is. Another emissary, this time a lord, arrives to ask when Hamlet will be ready for the match. The Prince replies that he awaits the King's pleasure. He is told that both King and Queen are now coming to witness the contest.

When the two are alone, Horatio warns Hamlet that he will lose the wager, but Hamlet replies that he does not think so, explaining that he has been in continual practice from the time Laertes left for France. Yet he concedes that he is heartsick — and then dismisses the thought as unmanly. Horatio urges him to postpone the match if he has any misgivings and offers to report that the Prince is indisposed. But Hamlet is resolute; he expresses his willingness to accept whatever is in store for him.

The King, the Queen, Laertes, Osric, and various attendants with foils and gauntlets enter. Next to Claudius' chair is a table on which are flagons of wine. Before taking his seat, the King puts Laertes' hand into that of Hamlet. Hamlet asks Laertes' pardon for having wronged him, stating that he had not intended any real harm but, sorely distracted, behaved as if he were out of his wits. Laertes replies stiffly that he bears no grudge against Hamlet as far as his personal feelings are concerned, but that he cannot accept the apology until experts in the matter of honor have proved to him that his reputation remains undamaged. Graciously, Hamlet accepts these conditions, asks that the foils be produced, and assures Laertes that he will serve as foil in the sense that Laertes will perform brilliantly in the duel. Laertes is sure that the Prince is mocking him, despite Hamlet's denial.

At Claudius' command, Osric brings the foils. While Laertes carefully chooses his, the King asks Hamlet if he knows about the wager. The Prince replies that Claudius is wagering on the weaker side, but the King assures him that he knows better, although the odds favor Laertes. Hamlet takes his foil, asking only whether or not it is the same length as the others. Before the contest starts, the King orders that, if Hamlet achieves the first or second hit, ordnance will be fired in his honor and the King himself will drink "to Hamlet's better breath." Moreover, he will place a precious pearl in the cup, which will belong to the duelist when he drinks to his own success. After the sound of kettledrums, trumpets, and the blast of cannons, Claudius drinks to Hamlet's health. The match begins.

Hamlet gets the first hit, and Claudius calls for the cup of wine, urging the Prince to drink and get the pearl he has won. But Hamlet wishes to continue the contest before drinking. Again he scores a hit, which is acknowledged by Laertes. During the short interval, Claudius remarks to Gertrude that their son will win. Gertrude expresses some doubt, remarking that Hamlet is out of condition. To the consternation of Claudius, she picks up the poisoned cup of wine which her husband has prepared for the Prince and drinks from it. She then offers it to Hamlet, who again refuses to drink. She offers to wipe his face. This brief interlude provides Laertes with the opportunity to reassure Claudius, but the King is no longer confident that Laertes will be able to score a hit upon Hamlet. Laertes himself, as his aside indicates (307), is struck at least momentarily with a sense of guilt.

The match is resumed. Laertes does wound Hamlet and in the scuffle between the two, the rapiers are exchanged. After they are parted, Hamlet is able to wound Laertes. At that very moment the Queen collapses. Horatio expresses his concern for the bleeding Hamlet, as Osric does for the bleeding Laertes. The Lord Chamberlain's son, aware that he is close to death, acknowledges that he is "justly kill'd with [his] own treachery" (318). When Hamlet cries out in concern for the Queen, Claudius replies that she has fainted at the sight of blood. But Gertrude survives just long enough to tell what has happened: "The drink, the drink! I am poison'd" (321).

Hamlet calls for the doors to be locked and demands that the treachery be exposed to the assembled members of the Court. Laertes then speaks up. He states that not only he, but also Hamlet, is near death and that the Prince now holds the "treacherous instrument" in his hand. Further, he declares that Gertrude has been poisoned and that the author of all this destruction is Claudius: "—the King, the King's to blame" (331). Hamlet lunges at Claudius, exclaiming, "Then, venom, to thy work" (334). The King survives only long enough to hear himself denounced by his nephew as the "incestuous, murderous, damn'd Dane" (333). Before dying, the contrite Laertes expresses his conviction that Claudius "is justly serv'd." He asks Hamlet's pardon, assuring the Prince that "Mine and my father's death come not upon thee,/Nor thine on me!"

Hamlet voices his wish that divine justice will absolve Laertes of any guilt and adds that he will follow Laertes in death. Turning to his dead mother, he bids the "wretched queen" farewell. He then implores Horatio to report all that happened fully and accurately so that there will be no misunderstandings after his death. But the faithful Horatio is ready to join Hamlet in death and is restrained only by the Prince's insistence that he survive to clear Hamlet's "wounded name."

The sounds of marching soldiers and a cannon shot are heard. Osric announces that young Fortinbras, fresh from conquest in Poland, has fired a salute in honor of the newly arrived English ambassadors. Hamlet lives just long enough to prophesy and to approve the election of Fortinbras as King of Denmark. Horatio speaks moving words of sorrow and tribute as Hamlet dies.

Fortinbras and the English ambassadors enter. The Norwegian Prince, used to bloodshed in battle, is shocked at the spectacle of death. The ambassadors, gazing on the "dismal" sight, are aware that the news which they were to bring to Claudius has arrived too late: they were to inform him that Rosencrantz and Guildenstern had been executed in accordance with his instructions. Horatio then speaks lines which go far toward summarizing the whole tragedy, the violent acts of which include adultery, murder, accidental deaths, deaths cunningly planned, and deaths which resulted from plans which went awry.

Fortinbras orders four captains to see to it that Hamlet is accorded full honors, including "soldiers' music and the rites of war."

Commentary

As he begins to fill in the details of what happened to him since he left Denmark, Hamlet concedes that "there was a kind of fighting" in his heart (4). But clearly his inner turmoil has been manifested from the time of his first appearance in this play. Now one is to hear no more expression of self-reproach or doubts that he will act positively against Claudius. What is impressive is his decisiveness. Thanks to what he calls "rashness" and "indiscretion," he is able to formulate a plan and to execute it without delay. As Samuel Johnson observed, Hamlet has found man's wisdom, or reason, to have its limitations: fortune, accident, chance—call it what one will—can determine the course of events, as his own experience aboard the ship proves. He was able to find in the dark the commission for his own death; by chance, he had in his possession his father's signet for sealing the forged document. No less by chance, the pirates proved "kind" and, for sufficient compensation, they returned him to Denmark.

"So Guildenstern and Rosencrantz go to't," says Horatio laconically (56). Some commentators read disapproval into his words. Certainly the deaths of these two servants of the King have led to much discussion. In Belleforest's non-dramatic version of *Hamlet*, both knew the contents of the commission; in Shakespeare's play, there is no evidence that Rosencrantz and Guildenstern knew that they were conducting the Prince to his death. As George Steevens, late eighteenth-century editor and critic of Shakespeare, remarked, "It is not [the critic's] office to interpret the plays of Shakespeare according to the novels on which they were founded—novels which the poet sometimes followed, but often materially deserted" *(New Variorum,* I, p. 420). If there is justification for Hamlet's action, then, it must be found in the text of the play. Was it a vindictive Hamlet who wrote that the two should be executed, no "shriving time allow'd" (47)? If so, he can hardly be said to have acted as one executing public justice rather than personal revenge. And it follows that, if indeed a divinity guided him at this time when, by his own testimony, he did not pause for thought, he functioned as God's scourge, not His minister.

But most commentators do not believe that Shakespeare intended so to denigrate the character of his tragic hero. If he makes Hamlet human enough to get grim satisfaction out of the fact that Rosencrantz and Guildenstern are not to be allowed time to purge their souls of sin, the essential point made by Hamlet is that there be no delay in the execution of the two and therefore no chance that the forgery would be discovered. More convincing is Horatio's reaction when Hamlet explains why "They are not near [his] conscience" (58-62). He insists that they loved their employment. One recalls that earlier he denounced them to their faces as sponges "that soak up the King's countenance" (IV.ii.16 ff.)—that is, they stood ready to do the King's every wish for the sake of personal reward. These two have been presented as servile half-men from the start. Rosencrantz and Guildenstern were surrogates of Claudius, Hamlet's mighty opposite. And of him, Horatio says, "Why, what a king is this!"

Yet it must be admitted that, after itemizing Claudius' major crimes, the Prince does not receive an answer to his question, one which is basic to his status as a moral symbol in the play:

> – is't not perfect conscience,
> To quit him with this arm? And is't not to be damn'd,
> To let this canker of our nature come
> In further evil?
>
> (67-70)

A. C. Bradley, among a few other critics, sees here a Hamlet who is still in doubt, still troubled by his conscience; and this view should not be ignored, if only because it illustrates once more the difficulties of interpretation. One may argue that there is no need for Horatio to answer Hamlet's question since he has already expressed deep shock at the latest evidence of Claudius' villainy. So, for many critics, the Hamlet in this scene has resolved all doubts; there is no longer "a kind of fighting" in his heart.

Of some significance is Hamlet's summary of Claudius' major offenses:

> He that hath kill'd my king and whor'd my mother,
> Popp'd in between th' election and my hopes,
> Thrown out his angle for my proper life. . . .
>
> (64-66)

First, there is no evidence of a fixation on an incestuous mother here, perhaps to the chagrin of the neo-Freudians. Second, although Hamlet has made reference to having an ambition to rule Denmark, he has done so primarily to mislead Claudius (See II.ii.259 ff; III.ii.97-99). Heretofore, the protagonist's ambition to rule Denmark has not been emphasized. Now he accuses his uncle of frustrating that ambition. Coming this late, however, the effect is not to transmute the play into an ambition tragedy. Claudius, however formidable as the antagonist to Hamlet, has been identified as a man notoriously inferior to the late King (See I.iv.8-12; II.ii.380-85). If Hamlet will perform a public duty in slaying Claudius, would it not be his duty also to prove himself to be his father's son by accepting the responsibilities of kingship? In experience, the young Prince has grown in stature since he spoke the lines of his first soliloquy and referred to both Claudius and himself in these words: "My father's brother, but no more like my father/Than I to Hercules" I.ii.152-53). He knows that he remains a mortal, but he knows also that he would not be "a king of shreds and patches."

When Horatio reminds Hamlet that Claudius is sure to learn soon what has happened to Rosencrantz and Guildenstern, Hamlet's reply (73-74) shows him to be controlled and confident. Now he expresses regret that he had so "forgot" himself as to offend Laertes, stating that he sees the image of his own cause in that of Ophelia's brother. Probably no more is intended than that Hamlet makes reference to the fact that both have endured great losses, for Hamlet's cause transcends the personal or domestic, involving as it does the welfare of the State. The Prince's determination to win back the goodwill of Laertes makes understandable his prompt agreement to participate in the fencing match.

Osric, a young courtier, brings to Hamlet the message from Claudius relating to the duel. A few lines would have sufficed for this purpose, but Shakespeare chose to present a full-length portrait of the fashionable, affected courtier, a familiar object of satire during the Renaissance. Hamlet identifies him as a "water-fly" – that is, an insect darting about the surface of water without any apparent purpose or reason – a busy trifler. Such lines as Hamlet's "Put your bonnet to his right use; 'tis for the head" (96) tell the reader how excessively formal Osric's gestures are. The courtier's style of discourse, burlesqued by the Prince, is marked by an overuse of Latinisms and elaborate metaphors. The attention which the poet-dramatist pays to Osric may be justified, at least to some extent, on the grounds that he serves to illustrate artificiality and pretense which characterize the Court, the leader of which is Claudius. But since both qualities have been well established already, some may conclude that the portrait of Osric is no more than a *tour de force* which the dramatist enjoyed creating.

"You will lose this wager, my lord," says Horatio after Osric has left (219). But Hamlet reassures his friend, saying that, while Laertes was in France, he (Hamlet) has "been in continual practice." One should not split hairs in the realm of critical commentary; nevertheless, some critics are reminded that the Prince himself had said that he had "forgone all custom of exercise" (II.ii.308). Later in the present scene, Gertrude will remark that her son is out of condition. Yet there is no question of Hamlet's skill as a swordsman. Ophelia's encomium described Hamlet as the ideal Prince and courtier – the accomplished Renaissance man, "The courtier's, soldier's, scholar's, eye, tongue, sword" (III.i.159).

Despite his confidence that he will "win at the odds," Hamlet concedes that he is heartsick (222-23). How could he be otherwise in view of all that has happened, and especially in view of the fact that, although Hamlet has been involved in violence, Claudius, the source of all rottenness, survives, ruling Denmark with Gertrude, the "imperial jointress"?

When Horatio urges him to consider withdrawing from the match, Hamlet makes reply in words weighty with import:

> . . . we defy augury. There's a
> special providence in the fall of a sparrow. If it be
> now, 'tis not to come; if it be not to come, it will
> be now; if it be not now, yet it will come; the
> readiness is all.
>
> (230-34)

What the Prince says here is consistent with what he said earlier in this scene when he declared that "There's a divinity that shapes our ends" (10). And if he is still heartsick, this passage provides additional evidence that no longer is there "a kind of fighting" in his heart—the kind that, early in the play, made him lament the fact that he was called upon to act violently because the "time is out of joint" (I.v.189-90), and later expend his energy in denunciation of his "mighty opposite" and accuse himself of inexcusable delay. Hamlet now seems to have resolved all doubts as to whether he functions as minister or as scourge. Finally, he no longer fears death or what may await him after death. When he says, "There's a special providence in the fall of a sparrow" (230-31), he is, of course, paraphrasing verses from the Bible—Matthew 10:28-31; Luke 12:4-7.

The "readiness is all." This dictum suggests that Hamlet has mastered passion. Inevitably it calls to one's mind his praise of Horatio as a man who is not passion's slave. Of him, the Prince said,

> for thou hast been
> As one, in suffering all, that suffers nothing,
> A man that Fortune's buffets and rewards
> Hath ta'en with equal thanks. . . .
>
> (III.ii.70-73)

Some students will remember that, in *King Lear*, Edgar, striving once more to win over his blind and oppressed father, the Earl of Gloucester, from despair, said:

> What, in ill thoughts again? Men must endure
> Their going hence even as their coming hither;
> Ripeness is all.
>
> (V.ii.9-11)

Gloucester, like Hamlet, would have welcomed death, although, unlike Hamlet, he was not restrained by conscience. He had lost faith in a supreme power or powers concerned with man's destiny. Thanks to the good offices of his son Edgar, he finally learns to accept Fortune's buffets with patience. In a word, he embraces Stoicism. Hamlet, who now knows that "readiness is all," has also embraced Stoicism. Curiously, at least one well-known Shakespearean editor and critic argues that Hamlet cannot become a Stoic, as Gloucester did, because Gloucester's world is pagan, not Christian as Hamlet's world is. Surely it is rather late to ignore the fact that Stoicism in its practical application to life had long since been Christianized in Western thought. Indeed there is a biblical echo in Edgar's words quoted above (cf. Job 14:12).

In his apology to Laertes, Hamlet is the soul of graciousness and sincerity. One remembers how he told Horatio how much he regretted his behavior in the graveyard (75-78). Nevertheless, there are certain disturbing elements in this episode preliminary to the fencing match. He tells Laertes that "madness" has been his enemy, yet again and again, from the time he told Horatio and members of the guard that he planned to adopt an "antic disposition," evidence has been presented to show that, however extravagant his words, and even his actions may have been on occasion, he was anything but demented. The conclusion to be made is that he refers here to that "kind of fighting" in his heart which led to emotional extremes. Certainly he has not "purpos'd evil"; but some critics find it strange that Hamlet makes no specific reference either to Polonius or to Ophelia. He merely asks Laertes to believe

> That I have shot mine arrow o'er the house
> And hurt my brother.
>
> (254-55)

Ironically, if Gertrude spoke truly when she said that she had hoped that Ophelia would have become Hamlet's wife (V.i.267), Laertes might have become the Prince's brother. "I'll be your foil," says Hamlet in the spirit of good fellowship (266), quibbling upon the word, which may mean "rapier" or "something which, by contrast, enhances a jewel." But, as things turn out, *Laertes* is the foil — in a far different sense.

No one is likely to underestimate the King as he appears during these preliminaries. From his first appearance in this play, he has demonstrated his skill at dissembling, presenting himself as the living embodiment of affability. It is he who places Laertes' hand in that of Hamlet; all hear him express absolute confidence in, and support of, his nephew. With an apparent abundance of goodwill, he promises Hamlet a princely reward. At his orders, martial music is sounded, and he drinks to Hamlet's success. Claudius is no ordinary villain; he is an accomplished one, the mighty opposite of the tragic hero. If Laertes were to wound Hamlet and survive unscathed, he alone would be aware of Claudius' fear and hatred of Hamlet.

Queen Gertrude is heard from only after the match has begun and Hamlet has scored the first hit with his blunted foil. No one should misinterpret her remark "He's fat, and scant of breath" (298), made just before she offers to wipe Hamlet's brow and prepares to drink to his success. Yet a few have managed to do just that, concluding that the Prince is corpulent. (A favorite theory, among this group, is that Richard Burbage, who created the role of Hamlet in the Elizabethan theater, had put on a bit too much weight in middle age.) But, as King James I is reported to have said, no melancholy man was ever fat. The context should tell even a modern critic that Gertrude is referring to the fact that Hamlet is perspiring, perhaps excessively—an indication, as she believes, that he is out of condition.

The action that follows is as exciting as any to be found in drama. Laertes is allowed to express twinges of conscience just before he wounds Hamlet; and, when he himself is fatally wounded, he has the good grace to acknowledge that his own treachery is responsible for his impending death. Moreover, just after the Queen cries out that she has been poisoned, he survives to place the blame upon Claudius. Demands of the plot at this point of its resolution, in part, explain Laertes' free confession and accusation. But it is not inappropriate that Laertes, who shortly before had declared that he stood aloof from Hamlet "in terms of honor" (258-60) and then faced the Prince armed with an unblunted and poisoned rapier, should be allowed to retrieve himself through full confession. Claudius must, and does, remain the villain of the piece.

"The point envenom'd too!" exclaims Hamlet at the moment of complete discovery, aware that he will soon join his mother and Laertes in death. One recalls that venom—poison—used by Claudius was the source of the rottenness in Denmark. It has spread throughout Elsinore and beyond. Polonius, Ophelia, and Rosencrantz and Guildenstern are among its victims.

At long last, Hamlet slays Claudius. The Prince survives not only to philosophize briefly on "this fell sergeant, Death," who is so "strict in his arrest" (347-48) but also, more important, to implore Horatio to report him and his cause aright—to clear his "wounded name." Certainly he does not want subjects of the Crown to believe that his slaying of Claudius was the latest and most shocking action of a Hamlet who, in the words of the First Gravedigger, was mad. Even less does he want to be remembered as the Pyrrhus-type of king-killer. Hamlet's concept of honor, implicit from the beginning, is something far above that held by Laertes and Polonius. He wishes to be remembered as the worthy son of the superior King Hamlet, as minister called upon to execute public justice, *not* as scourge. The moving words of Horatio, who knew him best, provide the best epitaph:

> Now cracks a noble heart. Good-night, sweet prince,
> And flights of angels sing thee to thy rest.
>
> (370-71)

For Hamlet was the "sweet prince"; and, in the Renaissance, the epithet *sweet* (like the adjective *gentle*) had special force, emphasizing superiority when applied to a person.

Fortinbras, who arrives near the very end of the play, also provides an epitaph:

> Let four captains
> Bear Hamlet, like a soldier, to the stage
> For he was likely, had he been put on,
> To have prov'd most royally....
>
> (406-9)

It is quite significant that Hamlet, who did not survive to rule Denmark (and in that sense had not "been put on"), is accorded a soldier's funeral. One is reminded again that the issue in the conflict between Hamlet and Claudius was a public one involving the health of the State.

In his dying words, Hamlet casts his vote for Fortinbras as the new ruler of Denmark. Fortinbras, one recalls, has been presented as one of the foils to Hamlet. Pointing out that the warlike Norwegian Prince, first determined to avenge his father's death, come what may, had listened to his royal uncle's reasoned argument and had turned his energies to a conquest of the Poles, some critics are sure that his ascension to the throne is especially fitting. According to their argument, Hamlet has paid the price for his inability to master passion before it was too late for him to avoid catastrophe (which in Renaissance high tragedy is always the death of the protagonist). Others, conceding that Hamlet failed in that he did not survive to prove himself his father's son as ruler of Denmark, insist that the very condition which made inevitable his failure, especially his unwillingness to act without much thought, is the measure of his greatness. For them, the Prince emerges finally as the sacrificial victim, one whose death is inevitable but which makes possible the purging of great evil and the restoration of a moral universe.

REVIEW QUESTIONS

1. In the "dram of evil" speech (I.iv.17 ff.) Hamlet advances three possible answers to the problem of evil. What are they? Is any one possibly applicable to Hamlet himself?
2. What particular passages in this drama provide one with a glimpse of the kind of young man Hamlet was before his crushing discovery of great evil?
3. What evidence may be adduced to indicate that Gertrude did not know how King Hamlet had met his death?

4. Why does Hamlet first believe in the "honesty" of the Ghost and then manifest profound doubts about its "honesty"? What is the significance here as regards (a) his character and (b) the major conflict in the play?

5. "How all occasions do inform against me," soliloquizes Hamlet after talking with Fortinbras' captain (IV.iv.32). Applying the term freely, what are the occasions which Hamlet believes reflect adversely on him?

6. What have the following to do with the main action and/or themes in this play?
    a. Hamlet's warm praise of Horatio (III.ii.59 ff.).
    b. Claudius' line: "How smart a lash that speech doth give my conscience!" (III.i.50).
    c. The selection from *Aeneas and Dido* recited by the players at Hamet's request (II.ii.490 ff.).

7. Rosencrantz and Guildenstern have been described as "half-men." What justification is there for that designation?

8. More than one character has been identified as being, in an important way, a foil to Hamlet. Who are two such characters, and in what way may each be considered as a foil to the protagonist?

9. Specifically, what are the sources of Hamlet's tragedy? Which do you consider to be most important? Why?

10. To what extent is the comic dialogue between the two Gravediggers in Act V, Scene i, functional rather than just a means of providing an amusing relief in the midst of serious action?

SELECTED BIBLIOGRAPHY

BRADLEY, A. C. *Shakespearean Tragedy*. Second edition. Macmillan, New York, 1949. Considers primary features of tragedy; the chapter on *Hamlet* develops the theory that the tragic hero falls as a result of melancholy; discusses Hamlet as an actual living person rather than as *dramatis persona*.

CAMPBELL, LILY B. *Shakespeare's Tragic Heroes: Slaves of Passion*. Cambridge University Press, 1930. Provides valuable background material on the purpose and method of tragedy, and the moral philosophy in Shakespeare's day; discusses *Hamlet* as a tragedy of the passion of excessive grief. As an historical relativist, she rejects the Bradley approach.

ELLIOT, G. R. *Scourge and Minister: A Study of Hamlet as a Tragedy of Revenge and Justice*. Duke University Press, Durham, N.C., 1951. Useful analysis of speeches and scenes.

FURNESS, H. H. *Hamlet. New Variorum Edition.* 2 Volumes. J. B. Lippincott, Philadelphia, 1877. Reprint, Dover Publications, 1963. Indispensable for earlier criticism and scholarship, and for textual study.

GRANVILLE-BARKER, HARLEY. *Prefaces to Shakespeare.* Vol. 1, Princeton University Press, 1946. Detailed discussion of the nature of the play, main lines of construction, characters and their interplay.

JOSEPH, BERTRAM. *Conscience and the King: A Study of Hamlet.* Chatto and Windus, London, 1953. Good discussion of the play from the theatrical point of view.

LEVIN, HARRY. *The Question of Hamlet.* Oxford University Press, New York, 1959. Basic for a grasp of the play's structure and style, as well as for exposition of the interrogative mode, doubt and irony, and the subject of madness.

PROSSER, ELEANOR. *Hamlet and Revenge.* Stanford University Press, 1968. Scholarly exposition of Christian elements in the play and a brilliant case for Hamlet as a tragic hero misled by the Ghost.

SCHÜCKING, L. L. *Character Problems in Shakespeare's Plays.* H. Holt, New York, 1922. Remains a stimulating and useful discussion of character problems in *Hamlet.*

TILLYARD, E. M. W. *Shakespeare's Problem Plays.* University of Toronto Press, 1950. Informed discussion of *Hamlet* as one of the problem plays.

WILSON, J. D. *What Happens in Hamlet.* Macmillan Company, 1935. Probably the best-known modern interpretation of *Hamlet;* especially useful for insights relating to individual scenes.

NOTES

Your Guides to Successful Test Preparation.

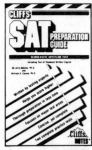  

Cliffs Test Preparation Guides

Efficient preparation means better test scores. Go with the experts and use **Cliffs Test Preparation Guides.** They'll help you reach your goals because they're: Complete • Concise • Functional • In-depth. They are focused on helping you know what to expect from each test. The test-taking techniques have been proven in classroom programs nationwide.

Recommended for individual use or as a part of formal test preparation programs.

TITLES		QTY.
2068-8	**ENHANCED ACT ($5.95)**	
2030-0	**CBEST ($7.95)**	
2040-8	**CLAST ($8.95)**	
1471-8	**ESSAY EXAM ($4.95)**	
2031-9	**ELM Review ($6.95)**	
2060-2	**GMAT ($7.95)**	
2008-4	**GRE ($6.95)**	
2065-3	**LSAT ($7.95)**	
2033-5	**MATH Review for Standardized Tests ($8.95)**	
2017-3	**NTE Core Battery ($14.95)**	
2020-3	**Memory Power for Exams ($4.95)**	
2044-0	**Police Sergeant Examination Preparation Guide ($9.95)**	
2032-7	**PPST ($7.95)**	
2002-5	**PSAT/NMSQT ($4.50)**	
2000-9	**SAT ($5.95)**	
2042-4	**TASP ($7.95)**	
2018-1	**TOEFL w/cassette ($14.95)**	
2034-3	**VERBAL Review for Standardized Tests ($7.95)**	
2041-6	**You Can Pass the GED ($9.95)**	

Prices subject to change without notice.
Available at your local bookseller or order by sending
the coupon with your check. **Cliffs Notes, Inc.,**
P.O. Box 80728, Lincoln, NE 68501.

Name _____
Address _____
City _____
State _____ **Zip** _____

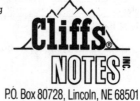

P.O. Box 80728, Lincoln, NE 68501

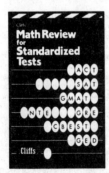